S.1.12   57362   Gift

D0811903

EDISON COMMUNITY COLLEGE
LIBRARY
1973 EDISON DR
PIQUA, OH 45356
937-778-8600

S.1.12   57362   Gift

A Higher Contemplation

57262

THE SACRED LANDMARKS SERIES
Michael J. Tevesz, Editor

The Sacred Landmarks Series includes both works of scholarship and general interest that preserve history and increase understanding of religious sites, structures, and organizations in Northeast Ohio, in the United States, and around the world.

A Higher Contemplation

Sacred Meaning in the Christian Art of the Middle Ages

Stephen N. Fliegel

Published in cooperation with Cleveland State University's College of Liberal Arts and Social Sciences

THE KENT STATE UNIVERSITY PRESS   KENT, OHIO

© 2012 by The Kent State University Press, Kent, Ohio 44242
All rights reserved
Library of Congress Catalog Card Number 2011000686
ISBN 978-1-60635-093-5
Manufactured in China

 Published in cooperation with Cleveland State University's
College of Liberal Arts and Social Sciences.

LIBRARY OF CONGRESS CATALOGING-IN-PUBLICATION DATA
Fliegel, Stephen N., 1950–
    A higher contemplation : sacred meaning in the Christian art of the Middle Ages /
Stephen N. Fliegel.
        p.   cm. — (Sacred landmarks series)
    "This book is an expanded and revised version of a mongraph titled Sacred
Meaning in the Christian Art of the Middle Ages published in 2004 by the Sacred
Landmarks Initiative at Cleveland State Univesity."
    Includes bibliographical references and index.
    ISBN 978-1-60635-093-5 (hardcover : alk. paper) ∞
    1. Christian art and symbolism—Medieval, 500-1500. I. Fliegel, Stephen N.,
1950- Sacred meaning in the Christian art of the Middle Ages. II. Title.
    N7850.F59 2011
    704.9'4820940902—dc22   2011000686

British Library Cataloging-in-Publication data are available.

15 14 13 12 11   5 4 3 2 1

Contents

The mortal man who beholds the image directs
his mind to a higher contemplation. His veneration is
no longer distracted . . . and art is able by means of colors
to ferry over the prayer of the mind.

—*the poet Agathias (ca. 532–582)*

Preface

This book is an expanded and revised version of a monograph titled *Sacred Meaning in the Christian Art of the Middle Ages* published in 2004 by the Center for Sacred Landmarks at Cleveland State University. The genesis of the monograph was a lecture that I gave on March 6, 2001, at Holy Trinity Church in Lorain, Ohio. The lecture was given at the invitation of Holy Trinity's pastor, Reverend David A. Novak, and was intended to serve as but a single element in a four-part lecture series that included other participants. The lecture series, "Images of Paradise," was organized and designed by Father Novak to examine the great traditions of Christian iconography and the connections between art and theology. I was honored to be included in that event and could never have imagined that my lecture would have evolved into the present publication.

Like the original lecture and subsequent monograph, this book is largely intended for the general reader. It is not intended to introduce new scholarship to an already rich corpus of literature on the subject. It is intended to introduce the subject of medieval Christian iconography— its forms, meaning, function, context, and symbolism—to the interested nonspecialist. Because much of the existing literature dealing with medieval Christian iconography takes the form of lexicons, encyclopedias, and dictionaries, the present publication is distinctive in that it approaches the subject as an illustrated narrative. I hope this book will have additional appeal to students, teachers, and those with an interest in religious art, Christian devotional practices, and the art and culture of the Middle Ages. Undoubtedly, all aspects of such a broad subject cannot be covered here, and I would encourage my readers to use the bibliography to access more in-depth and focused sources of information. It is my hope that this book will introduce the reader to the subtleties, complexities, richness, range, and antiquity of these medieval Christian artistic traditions and the multiple levels within which they can be experienced. Some of the most profound and enduring works of art in Western civilization were produced for private devotion or public worship. Indeed, many of the most significant artists of the Middle Ages and Renaissance earned their livelihood in the service of the church and the production of religious art. I therefore hope that readers will be further motivated to explore the copious literature dealing with the subject. I am also hopeful that readers will discover anew the rich heritage of medieval European art, defined over the span of a millennium, and the more recent Christian art and architecture, which draws their forms and inspiration from medieval European art. Knowledge, I believe, enhances appreciation.

Astute readers will note that many of the illustrations in this book derive from the distinguished collection of medieval art at the Cleveland Museum of Art, though I have drawn from many other sources as well. Having served as curator of the Cleveland medieval collection for many years, I have used in this book works of art that I am familiar with, that in some instances are among the finest of their type, and that illustrate the points expressed in my text.

The medieval collection at the Cleveland Museum of Art consists of works produced in continental Europe, the British Isles, and the eastern Mediterranean basin during the period spanning the third century A.D. through the early 1500s. Included are works of art produced in a variety of materials, techniques, and styles, gathered largely as a collection of masterpieces rather than as an attempt to illustrate the whole of medieval civilization.

In 1920 J. H. Wade II established a trust fund enabling the purchase of Medieval Art at the Cleveland Museum of Art. In 1931 Cleveland Museum of Art director William Milliken was able to purchase eight pieces, thanks to the Wade fund, from the *Guelph Treasure*, a famous ensemble consisting of 85 sacred objects from the Cathedral of Saint Blaise, in Brunswick, north Germany, named for the family that established the collection. These pieces contributed significantly to the Cleveland Museum of Art's status as a world-class museum and an important repository of works of medieval art. Milliken, who retired in 1958, subsequently added other works of high quality and historical significance to the medieval collection, such as the unique gothic table fountain and the alabaster mourners from the tombs of the dukes of Burgundy. William D. Wixom, Cleveland Museum of Art's curator of medieval art 1958–78, continued to build the collection with additions such as the "Jonah Marbles" and the "Hours of Queen Isabella the Catholic."

In June 1916 Cleveland's new art museum opened its front doors for the first time, revealing among its newly acquired treasures a breathtaking installation of European arms and armor resplendent with colorful regimental banners and a set of magnificent seventeenth-century Flemish tapestries. This installation would evermore designate the museum's signature space, the "Armor Court." The collection truly became one of the most cherished and revered spaces in Cleveland, all due to the munificence of Mr. and Mrs. John L. Severance's gift of funds to purchase an extensive collection of arms and armor. Although the size of the medieval collection is relatively small (about 1,500 objects), it includes sculptures, ivories, enamels, paintings, manuscripts, tapestries, and pieces of armor and weaponry of world-class quality and importance.

Readers of this book, regardless of where they live, most likely have access to fine collections of medieval art. In addition to the Cleveland Museum of Art, there exist exceptional major collections of medieval art in the United States at the Metropolitan Museum of Art, the Cloisters, and the Pierpont Morgan Library in New York; the Museum of Fine Arts, Boston; the Walters Art Museum, Baltimore; the J. Paul Getty Museum, Los Angeles; the Detroit Art Institute; the Toledo Museum of Art; and the Chicago Art Institute. Smaller American collections of medieval art with quality holdings exist in other cities.

Europeans and foreign visitors to Europe will, of course, have access to medieval art *in situ* in the many churches and cathedrals, chapels, and palaces across the continent. Great national collections of medieval art exist in many of Europe's major museums such as the British Museum, the British Library, and the Victoria and Albert Museum in London. In Paris, the Louvre and the Cluny Museum preserve highly important collections, as do the Kunstgewerbemuseum in Berlin, the Bavarian National Museum in Munich, the Prado in Madrid, and the Bargello in Florence. These are merely a few of the many troves of medieval sculpture, paintings, textiles, and small objects in large and small cities across Europe. Interested readers are encouraged to seek these works of art, many of which are illustrated here. I hope that this book brings enjoyment in that process of discovery and that it opens windows to the greater understanding of these magnificent works of art and the rich artistic legacy of the European Middle Ages.

Acknowledgments

I am deeply indebted to my good friend Father David A. Novak, who invited me to participate in the "Images of Paradise" lecture series. Without him, this book would have never been realized. Nor would the earlier monograph and this book have been published without the interest, warm support, and encouragement of another friend, Dr. Michael J. Tevesz, director of the Center for Sacred Landmarks at Cleveland State University and general editor of this series. I wish to express my deepest gratitude to Dr. Tevesz, without whom this book would not exist. I am also grateful to Douglas Hoffman, who read an early draft of my manuscript and suggested changes. At the Kent State University Press, I wish to thank Will Underwood, director; Joyce Harrison, acquiring editor; Mary Young, managing editor; and the editorial board. At the Cleveland Museum of Art, I would like to thank Amanda Mikolic, curatorial assistant in medieval art, for her assistance with image procurement and rights. For the superb drawings that appear at the end of this book and that lend illustration to the glossary, I would like to thank graphic artist Carolyn Lewis.

STEPHEN N. FLIEGEL
Curator of Medieval Art
The Cleveland Museum of Art

CHAPTER ONE

The Context and the Medieval Mind

Images are the books of the unlettered. For what the Scripture teaches
those who read, this same the image shows to those who cannot read
but see.

   —Pope Gregory the Great (540–604)

e inhabit today, in the West at least, a pluralistic society
in which all faiths and their respective cultural traditions
have relative merit. Moral and political hegemony is not
restricted to a single belief system, and tolerance is a basic tenet of our society. Yet a millennium ago, Europe was not so diverse. Christianity was the
unifying principle of the Middle Ages. From Scandinavia to Ethiopia, daily
life, culture, law, and every other aspect of civilization were drawn from the
same Christian source. Within this broadly Catholic tradition there coexisted
many different cultural approaches to the religious experience. At its epicen-
ter, however, was the role of religious art. This art provided a visual language
that would have been as equally recognizable in the Egyptian desert as in
the towns of the Baltic. The association of sacred images with ecclesiastical
architecture is so profound that even in today's secular society the expecta-
tion on entering a church is to encounter a physical artistic representation of
Christ, the Virgin Mary, the angels, or saints. These images, fashioned from
various materials, might assume the form of monumental sculpture, stained
glass, painting, metalwork, or something as delicate as an ivory panel, a small
enamel plaque, or a textile. What may not be readily apparent to the modern
viewer is the great antiquity of this tradition. Its history reaches back across
the centuries to the dawn of Christianity (fig. 1).

Figure 1 (facing page). *Icon of the Mother of God*. Tapestry, wool (70⅜ x 43½ in.). Egypt (Byzantine Period), 6th century. The Cleveland Museum of Art. Purchase, Leonard C. Hanna Jr. Bequest 1967.144

Figure 2. *Christ of the Last Judgment*. Drawing, pen and ink (26 x 18.5 cm). Martin Schongauer, German (1435–91). Musée du Louvre, Paris, Inv. 18785. (Photo Credit: Réunion des Musées Nationaux/Art Resource, NY)

Also escaping the attention of the modern viewer are the various shades of meaning implied by the form, placement, color, and juxtaposition of these images. This Christian artistic vocabulary emerged over time, through trial, error, and design, during the European Middle Ages. By the end of this epoch, about 1500, an established repertory of Christian sacred images and symbols had been defined. This iconography, this sacred vocabulary, is the very essence—the heart and soul—of medieval art. It can be found in the involved sculptural programs of Europe's great cathedrals, in the painted altarpieces that graced their interiors, and within the pages of illuminated manuscripts, both liturgical and devotional. Biblical history is revealed within great expanses of stained glass some forty feet high or within an object so small that it fits in the hand.

The implications for medieval artists and their patrons were significant. A veritable sacred dogma consisting of artistic principles had evolved and was supervised by the church. When it came to representing Christ, the Virgin, and the saints, little was left to the individual whim of the artist (fig. 2). Established artistic conventions were learned and memorized by artists from one end of Europe to the other, and failure to submit to these conventions would have been tantamount to heresy at the worst or would have resulted in a lack of commissions and the end of careers at the very least.

If we are to access these images today and understand their nuances, we must know something of the medieval social condition and the texture of those times. In the early twenty-first century, our world is many times different from that experienced by medieval men and women. Sensory overload from computers, cell phones, television, cinema, radio, billboards, and so forth has to some degree desensitized the modern viewer of traditional artistic expression. The Middle Ages knew silence and darkness in their purest forms. Few of us today can know the experience of a night sky undiluted by city lights or total silence free of the sounds of traffic and passing aircraft. Europe in the Middle Ages was very different. Their world knew the experience of pitch darkness and stark silence. Consequently the visual impact of a sculpted cathedral tympanum or a blaze of stained glass would have impressed and moved the viewer in a way now difficult to imagine. The emotional response to a sacred image would have been very profound.

The eminent Dutch historian Johann Huizinga has described this environment in his classic work, *The Waning of the Middle Ages*.[1] Huizinga in his singularly elegant prose noted that the medieval town did not lose itself in continuous outlying suburbs. It constituted a well-defined entity, walled with gates for defense. Towns could, and did, lock themselves up at night by bolting their gates shut, an act that was emblematic of the medieval psyche. The Middle Ages was a period of extremes, of stark contrasts between compassion and unspeakable cruelty, between beauty and squalor, between power and helplessness, between wealth and poverty. One of the greatest images in Western art that captures the sublime medieval appreciation for basic shelter and warmth is the February calendar scene from Jean de Berry's *Très Riches Heures* of about 1412–16 (fig. 3).[2] The miniature shows the starkness of the northern winter. As Huizinga expressed it, "We at the present day, can hardly understand the keenness with which a fur coat, a good fire on the hearth, a soft bed, a glass of wine, were formerly enjoyed."[3]

Our stereotypes of medieval men and women have no doubt been defined by film and fiction and by the sometimes sterile environment of the museum setting. In contrast to the sparse and monochromatic ambience of medieval churches today, religious experience in the Middle Ages often was shaped by colorfully painted walls, ceilings, and sculpture. The devotee would be exposed to glittering gold and silver reliquaries and liturgical objects often studded with gemstones, which provided a visual focus to the Mass and the veneration of the saints. Unfortunately, extant medieval sculptures have often lost their rich polychromy, and medieval churches their gilding, paint,

Figure 3. *Calendar: February* from *Les Très Riches Heures.* Ink, tempera, and gold on vellum (29 x 21 cm). Limbourg Brothers, France, ca. 1412–16. Musée Condé, Chantilly MS 65/1284, fol. 2v. (Photo Credit: Réunion des Musées Nationaux/Art Resource, NY)

and frescoes. What is essential to recall is that the medieval world was not chromatically neutral or bland. Medieval men and women loved bright color. They inhabited a chromatic environment in which color invoked passion, mystery, meaning, and joy. Modern films about the Middle Ages would have

Figure 4. *Calendar: October* from *Les Très Riches Heures*. Ink, tempera, and gold on vellum (29 x 21 cm). Limbourg Brothers, France, ca. 1412–16. Musée Condé, Chantilly MS 65/1284, fol. 10v. (Photo Credit: Réunion des Musées Nationaux/Art Resource, NY)

Figure 5. *Procession of the Blessed Sacrament.* Fol. 43v. from the *Book of Hours of Queen Isabella the Catholic.* Ink, tempera, and gold on vellum (22.5 x 15.2 cm), ca. 1497–1500. Alexander Bening and Associates, Flemish, Ghent, ca. 1444–1519. The Cleveland Museum of Art. Purchase, Leonard C. Hanna Jr. Bequest 1963.256

us believe that medieval people wore drab brown and gray clothes, that the peasants were continuously mud-caked, and that their world was relatively somber. The miniatures in medieval manuscripts tell us a different story. Men and women—even peasants—are shown wearing colorful tunics, as exemplified by the October scene of tilling and sowing in *Les Très Riches Heures* (fig. 4).[4] The Middle Ages had developed a broad range of organic and mineral dyes. The men and women of that time simply loved color.

Some of us may suffer the illusion that medieval people were less intelligent than we are today. That, however, was not the reality. They may have been less knowledgeable, because knowledge is cumulative, but they were certainly no less intelligent than us. Were they more emotional, however? Absolutely. Everything we know about medieval men and women and the tenor of their times suggests that they were easily moved to tears. They could be provoked to cry at almost any stimulus—a religious procession winding its way through the streets of a town (fig. 5), a coronation, a royal birth, an execution, a cleric's sermon, or a religious image, for example.

A modern observer transported back in time to the Middle Ages would notice the frequent, rhythmic, almost continuous peal of bells. This is the one sound above all others that pierced the relative silence of their world. And this too, on certain occasions, elicited deep emotions. Bells gave medieval life structure. Small villages had their parish church, which had a small bell tower to summon the faithful to Mass. The larger cities—Paris, Cologne, London, and Rome—included many parish churches, plus their great cathedrals and conventual churches belonging to the different religious orders, including the Dominicans, the Franciscans, the Carthusians, and the Augustinians. The bells of all these churches supplied each day with its rhythm, marking the eight canonical hours. These devotions would have started at approximately 2:30 A.M. with the office of matins, then continued with lauds, prime, terce, sext, none, vespers, and compline. This was the structure of daily life. Bells also announced the great occasions, such as the death of a king, the election of a pope, or the birth of a prince. Bells announced the calamities of life, like pestilence, floods, fire, and warfare.

Into this world, in which much of the population remained illiterate, the impact of sacred images on the churchgoer was profound. "I am a poor ignorant woman; I cannot read. Inside my village church I see Paradise painted . . . and Hell, where the damned are boiled. One frightens me, the other gives me joy."[5] These words were written by the fifteenth-century French poet François Villon, who, in the guise of a fictional character, spoke for the illiterate masses of medieval Europe. For them, sacred art became a kind of pictorial sermon. By the end of the Middle Ages, churches were replete with sacred images produced in a variety of media. In *Les Très Riches Heures*, the miniature of *The Holy Sacrament*, painted by Jean Colombe between 1485 and 1489, shows the interior space of an ornate church (fig. 6).[6] The viewer sees a number of sculptures surmounting elaborately carved columns within and above a balducchino surrounding the high altar. Above and beyond, the viewer witnesses large, glazed spaces filled with stained glass. Here undoubtedly were dozens of individual scenes of biblical history, Gospel events, the Apocrypha, the life of the Virgin, the Passion and Crucifixion of Christ, and the lives of the saints.

Figure 6. *The Holy Sacrament* from *Les Très Riches Heures.* Ink, tempera, and gold on vellum (29 x 21 cm). Jean Colombe, Bourges, ca. 1482. Musée Condé, Chantilly MS 65/1284, fol. 129v. (Photo Credit: Réunion des Musées Nationaux/Art Resource, NY)

The function and placement of religious sculpture in context can be staggering. Sculpture was used for altarpieces, behind altars, above or near altars, as reliquaries, as movable images, for choir screens, on pulpits and lecterns, for piers or niches, on building exteriors, on holy water fonts, on tombs, on roadside shrines, and for private devotion in the home.[7] In addition to the

Figure 7. *Vesperbild (Pietà)*. Polychromed and gilded lindenwood (H. 89 cm). Master of Rabenden, German, Bavaria, active ca. 1510–1530. The Cleveland Museum of Art, Purchase from the J. H. Wade Fund 1938.294

obvious didactic function of religious images, they also filled another need of both the beholder and the church: veneration—candles were lit before the sacred images (fig. 7). They were censed. Offerings were made in the name of the figures represented, and they were honored and cherished in a very direct way. Images also served to remind viewers of the pious and virtuous lives of the saints and their sacrifices and to aid in meditation. Finally, sacred images served to embellish the sacred space and to give it luster.[8]

Sacred art was an important ingredient in the formative power and energy of medieval piety. A number of medieval accounts, whether legendary or factual, and some of them dealing with famous individuals, refer to the presence of an image as a critical element in the visionary experiences of saints and mystics. These stories often refer to artistic images of Christ, the Virgin, or the saints suddenly coming to life. Evidence of the influence of such artistic images may be found in the experiences of the mystical elite—Dame Julian of Norwich, Margaretha Ebner, Saints Catherine of Alexandria, Hildegard von

Bingen, and Catherine of Siena, for example. To understand this art today, we must bear in mind the context, the intended audience, and its functionality in the public or private space.

Images of sacred persons could be both portable and intimate. For example, a fourteenth-century ivory diptych from Germany (fig. 8), essentially two carved panels hinged at the center, illustrates the immediacy that could be achieved by sacred art. When open, the diptych exposed four scenes from the life of Christ. Little is known about how such objects functioned as votive objects in the fourteenth century. Most likely it was kept closed when not in use. Was it stored in a small box or casket? We don't know. When the owner wished to pray or meditate, he or she would have stood it open on a small table or prie-dieu, perhaps covered in velvet, so that he or she could fixate on the images as worthy subjects of devotion. Possibly the owner lit candles

Figure 8. *Diptych with Scenes from the Life of Christ.* Ivory (20.7 x 22.3 cm). Germany, ca. 1375. The Cleveland Museum of Art, The Andrew R. and Martha Holden Jennings Fund 1984.158, a&b

before it to create a suitable atmosphere for meditation and to honor the images. The diptych was presumably an expensive object; ivory was a luxury generally available only to those who could afford to purchase a ready-made diptych from a shop or, more likely, commission such an object from an artist. The four images carved into this ivory should be read left to right then top to bottom. In this way it reveals sequentially the following scenes: (1) the raising of Lazarus, (2) the entry into Jerusalem, (3) the Crucifixion, and (4) the entombment of Christ. These images, striking for their small size and for the bold quality of their workmanship, are incisively rendered with great vivacity and naturalism of poses and gestures. This may be observed in the swooning Virgin at the foot of the cross, or the charmingly rendered detail of the child in the palm tree handing a branch to Christ as his companions divest themselves of their cloaks for use as carpets for the Savior as he reaches the gates of Jerusalem. Not only do these scenes illustrate the death of the Redeemer for the sins of mankind but also, through the image of Lazarus, they reveal the potential for resurrection and eternal life in all men and women. The placement and juxtaposition of these individual scenes suggest a conscious choice on the part of someone. A choice of images representing Christ's life, Passion, death, and resurrection would have been available to the patron who commissioned this object, and yet there is a choice of specific subjects for these images within the broader matrix of themes.

In the case of this ivory diptych, the essential point is that ivory carvers of the fourteenth century, much like the illuminators of psalters and books of hours, brought into the private domain images that only a century earlier were restricted to public places. While the image remained the same as that experienced in a church or chapel, crafted in ivory its function was now radically different. In the case of the sculpted or painted scene in the church, the choice of scenes to be included was inevitably made by a group of clerics who wanted to express certain theological ideas or invoke specific didactic intentions. For the owner of ivory, probably a layperson, the choice of scenes indicates which images the patron wished to have before him or her during meditation. It is therefore an expression of individual preference and individual piety. While the same image in a church could be experienced simultaneously by many people, the ivory was made for the private devotions of a single person. A pious patron would come to regard these four specific scenes as the most important moments of God's redemptive relationship with him or her.

Yet the use of sacred images and artistic embellishments in the medieval Christian context was not without its critics. Bernard of Clairvaux (1090–1153), spiritual head of the reformed Cistercian order and one of the most influential figures of the twelfth century, took notable issue with the use of enrichments and ornamentation to the ecclesiastical space. "What is beautiful is more admired than what is holy," he complained.[9] Bernard saw a danger

in valuing what is beautiful and edifying in a work of art. He viewed the use of sculpture, stained glass, and painting as a profound distraction to the principal focus of Christian prayer and contemplation.

Figure 9. *Church of San Galgano, Italy.* Aerial view of the ruins. 13th century. (Photo Credit: Alinari/Art Resource, NY)

Any discussion of sacred meaning in Christian art must address certain points concerning the place of architecture in the religious and theological cosmos. As with sculptors and painters, builders and architects similarly followed a set of principles in erecting an ecclesiastical structure. The idea that a church building could serve a didactic purpose extends to the earliest churches, those of Late Antiquity. By the Gothic age, cathedral architecture had become a veritable intellectual system. Churches were identified with the Virgin, the community of saints, the Old and New Testaments, the second coming of Christ, and other themes through a broad and sophisticated range of visual cues. The church building, as a work of architecture, was designed to convey a precise message to its immediate audience. Through its shape and orientation, as well as its images, it functioned as a teaching tool. The architectural frame was therefore both the bearer of images and the bearer of meaning.

Churches have traditionally been designed and aligned in a prescribed manner. Most significant is the cruciform shape of the building itself (fig. 9). While in modern Christian churches this is seldom observed, during the Middle Ages, churches—from the smallest to the grandest—were nearly always shaped like a cross with nave, choir, transepts, and crossing. Additionally, they were aligned with the altar facing east. It was held that at the Second Coming, Christ would

arrive from the East. Thus, the east end of a church (the upper vertical arm in the cruciform plan occupied by the choir or sanctuary), with the high altar and a great expanse of stained glass windows, would capture the first rays of the morning sun—an appropriate symbol of Christ's coming.

Each of the four cardinal points of a cruciform church is therefore aligned with the principal points of the compass. The north transept faced the land of cold and dark—the North. This area of the church was symbolically dedicated to the Old Testament, the old law. The south transept, facing the area of warmth and sunlight, was dedicated to the New Testament, representing the new law. The west end represented that area of the church that would capture the last rays of the setting sun on the last day of the world. It was therefore dedicated to the Last Judgment.

The Gothic cathedral may be considered an intellectual system. Numbers and symmetry were very important in ecclesiastical architecture. The Middle Ages possessed a great appreciation of order, structure, and harmony. All of humanity's endeavors were appropriately held to these principles, whether scholarship, writing, music, the visual arts, or architecture—they thus were a reflection of divine perfection. Numerology, the study of the meaning of numbers, held great sway with the academics and theologians of the period. The number one signified the one God; two, the dual nature of Christ, who was both human and divine. Three was, of course, the Holy Trinity. Four represented the Four Evangelists, the four greater prophets, or the four seasons. Five represented the Five Wounds of Christ. Seven had great significance, representing the seven sacraments, the seven last words, the seven deadly sins, the seven sorrows of the Virgin, the seven liberal arts, and so on. These rules and implied symbols were applied to buildings so that the number of doors, windows, towers, and other architectural elements were held to have significance. Common features of the Gothic cathedrals that emerged during the twelfth and thirteenth centuries were triple portals, twin towers, and a single rose window on the west end (fig. 10). The rules of numerology and symmetry were applied and read with great avidity during the Middle Ages.

Figure 10. *West Facade of Reims Cathedral,* after 1254. (Photo Credit: Scala/Art Resource, NY)

CHAPTER TWO

The Early Christian and Byzantine Perception of Images

The subject of sacred imagery in the period represented from the early Christians through the Renaissance poses certain challenges to the modern viewer. First is the time scale involved, which spans roughly one and a half millennia, the first three-quarters of the Christian era. This is a substantial period of time in which Christian ideas, images, and doctrines were formed and defined. We must now ask the question, how would the faithful recognize these sacred persons and the great biblical events represented in ecclesiastical and devotional art? And finally, what is the origin of this iconography? Early Christian art was profoundly ideological. It was also an art that was meant to be gazed at long and passionately. Christianity appeared at the end of the reign of Tiberius—about 37 A.D. It was feared by the Roman state, condemned under Nero in 64 A.D., and persecuted for the next two and a half centuries. The first Christian artists adopted many pagan pictorial themes from the classical culture of Rome, eliminating the idolatrous or sensual images and interpreting them with a secret symbolism. Christian art was not an original creation. It derived from Roman and Near Eastern art—from semi-Oriental, semi-Hellenistic cities like Alexandria, Antioch, and Ephesus.

Initially, Christians inherited a mistrust of realistic figural images from Judaism, rooted in an intrinsic fear of idolatry. However, in spite of this mistrust, some Christians were actively promoting and sanctioning biblical im-

ages by the third century. At the end of the century, a veritable system of religious iconography had been formed. By the middle of the sixth century, most Christians were no longer so mistrustful of images. Not only did they commission portraits of Christ but they showed them the veneration that previously had been reserved for portraits of emperors. The first Christian artists were faced with serious questions: How do you imagine God? Should images of Christ show him as young and beardless or with long, dark hair and a curling beard? As late as the sixth century, Christ was still occasionally depicted beardless, as in a mosaic from the Church of San Vitale, Ravenna (fig. 11). Or conversely, should Christ be represented symbolically as a lamb or a fish? How would a Christian recognize a saint if he or she appeared to him in a dream? What shape should a church be? And inside, what forms of decoration are appropriate? Questions like these confronted artists and their patrons of the early Christian and Byzantine world. The solutions they devised are visible to us today in museums and churches around the world.

Early Christian artists developed a visual language of symbols. Among frequently recurring motifs in early Christian art are the peacock, the dove, the

Figure 11. *Christ, Angels, Saint Vitalis and Bishop Ecclesius.* Apse mosaic, 6th century. Church of San Vitale, Ravenna. (Photo Credit: Cameraphoto Arte, Venice/ Art Resource, NY)

Figure 12. *Floor Mosaic Panel: Grape Harvester with a Peacock.* Marble tesserae. Byzantium, Northern Syria, 5th century. The Cleveland Museum of Art. John L. Severance Fund 1969.112

palm, the fish, the grapevine, and the lamb. The dove was both a reminder of Noah's deliverance from the flood and a symbol of the Holy Ghost, and the palm of victory denoted the martyr's triumph over death. Many of these motifs appear for the first time in the context of Christian funerary art of the second century after Christ, the most obvious being wall paintings within the catacombs. For a Christian, the peacock, with its supposedly incorruptible flesh, symbolized immortality. Such symbols abound in the early Christian repertory. A floor mosaic, for example, originally from a fifth-century north Syrian church and now in the Cleveland Museum of Art, shows a peacock together with a grape harvester (fig. 12). Symbolically, the *Grape Harvester with a Peacock* conveys well-known Christian themes. The grapes represent the Eucharistic wine and thus the blood of Christ, while the peacock symbolizes immortality.

A sixth-century panel from an altar frontal (fig. 13) is also clearly embellished with Christian symbols. This relief sculpture derives its inspiration from sarcophagus iconography in early Byzantium and is highly typical in ornamentation of those produced in the Italian city of Ravenna during the sixth century. After 540 Ravenna became the seat of the Byzantine governors of Italy and is still remarkable for its basilicas and mausoleums, many of which contain unique cycles of mosaics. Like most early Byzantine sarcophagi, this altar frontal relief depends on an arrangement of arches, pediments, and classical

Figure 13. *Altar Frontal.* Marble. Byzantium, Ravenna, ca. 540–600. The Cleveland Museum of Art. John L. Severance Fund 1948.25

columns, as well as a vocabulary of symbols commonly found in early Christian art. These include scallop shells, lambs, palms, and crosses to symbolically represent the concepts of life, the sacrifice of Christ, victory over death, and eternal life. The altar frontal to which this relief belonged was originally in the Church of San Carlino (formerly the Church of Santi Fabiano e Sebastiano) in Ravenna. In its original form it might have been carved on all four sides with an arched roof. The sarcophagus was altered during the 1700s during renovations in the church. At that time, the sarcophagus panel was converted into an altar frontal. The lower part of the curtains and the marble between them were cut away to form a receptacle with grating to guard the relics of the two saints, Fabian and Sebastian. Originally, this relief would have contained a carved cross or a monogram of Christ between the curtains.

Among the earliest and most compelling survivors from Late Antiquity is a group of five symbolic early Christian sculptures now preserved in the Cleveland Museum of Art (fig. 14). The ensemble, popularly called the Jonah Marbles, is unique among Late Antiquity sculpture in the round for its Christian subject matter. The group consists of four marble figures (*Jonah Swallowed, Jonah Cast Up, Jonah Praying,* and *Jonah under the Gourd Vine*) taken from the story of Jonah and a fifth representing the *Good Shepherd*. When introduced publicly in 1965, this sculptural ensemble astonished the art world not only for its superb quality and condition but also for its very survival. If only one of these sculptures had survived, it would have been truly amazing. That all five survived the vicissitudes of time—seventeen centuries, in fact—and are still preserved together is nothing short of miraculous.

The Jonah Marbles all appear to share a common origin: the entire group was purportedly unearthed from a large *pithos,* or jar. Unfortunately, its original location was not recorded and remains unknown. That the sculptures

Figure 14. *Group of Early Christian Sculptures ("The Jonah Marbles")*. Marble. Asia Minor, probably Phrygia (Central Turkey), ca. 270–280 A.D. The Cleveland Museum of Art. John L. Severance Fund 1965.237– 1965.241

belonged together is supported by their common material, similarities of style and execution, and burial accretions over their surfaces. Recent isotopic analysis of the marble from which the sculptures were carved points to the Roman Imperial quarries at Dokimeion in ancient Phrygia, now Central Turkey, as the source of this marble. The Dokimeion quarries supplied the Roman Empire with highly prized, quality marble, which was fashioned from unfinished blocks into sculpture, paving, and veneer. This finding, of course, does not prove the sculptures were actually carved in this area. However, careful study of the sculptural style of the Jonah Marbles reinforces their probable genesis in this part of the late Roman world.

Christians adopted *The Good Shepherd* (fig. 15) at an early date to represent Christ as the savior of his Christian flock. So familiar is the shepherd in early Christian art that it is easy to lose sight of its pagan origin. Yet, in Greece the *Hermes Criophorus* (the ram carrier or calf bearer) is known very early as a subject for sculpture, and its "adoption" by Christians would probably have passed unnoticed by pagan neighbors. Thus, in catacomb paintings or floor mosaics, the Good Shepherd symbolizes deliverance as prefigured in Psalm 23. The Gospel reference that first comes to mind is the parable of the Good Shepherd in John (10:11–16). However, in early Christian art the shepherd is more likely derived from the reference in Luke (15:4–7) to the finding of one lost sheep in the hundred in the flock: "And when he hath found it, he layeth it on his shoulders, rejoicing. . . . I say unto you, that likewise joy

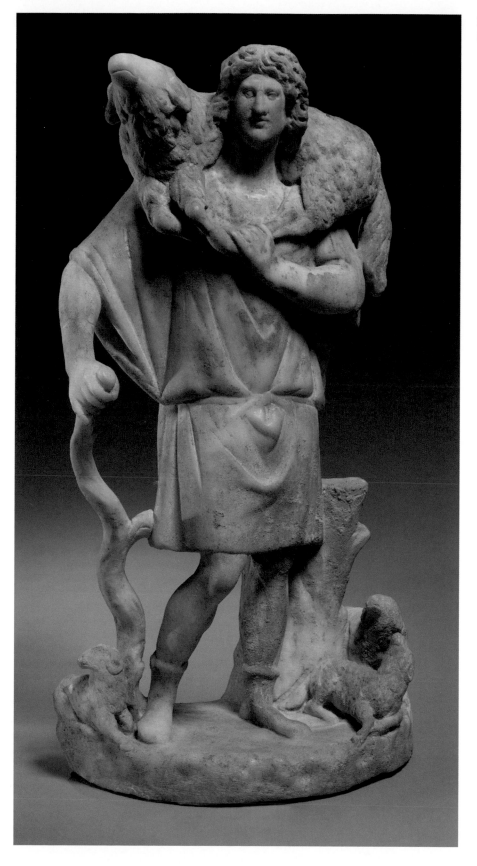

Figure 15. *The Good Shepherd.*
(H. 19½ in.). 1965.241

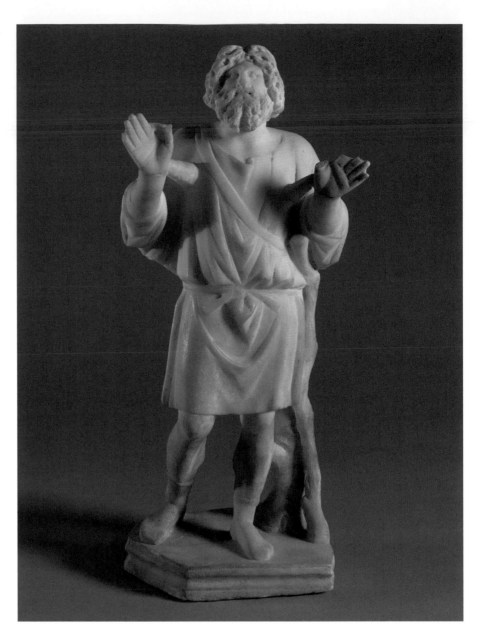

Figure 16. *Jonah Praying.* (H. 18½ in.). 1965.240

shall be in heaven over one sinner that repenteth, more than over ninety and nine just persons which need no repentance." In truth, numerous small-scale, freestanding marble sculptures of the Good Shepherd survive from Late Antiquity. What makes the Cleveland *Good Shepherd* so special is its artistic quality, its condition, its Hellenized style, and especially its place within a larger ensemble of religious sculptures.

The four figures of Jonah depict incidents from the well-known biblical story (see fig. 14). Swallowed by a "great fish" for his disobedience to God, Jonah spent three days in the beast's stomach. After repenting, he was disgorged unharmed. The four Jonah sculptures, like that of the *Good Shepherd*, conform to a language of symbols developed by the early Christians. They make reference to resurrection, life after death, and salvation. *Jonah Swallowed* and *Jonah Cast Up* were understood by early Christians to represent the death and resurrection of Christ. The Gospel of Matthew (12:40) reads: "For as Jonah was three days and three nights in the whale's belly; so shall the Son of Man be three days and three nights in the heart of the earth." In the biblical story of Jonah, the gourd vine, under which Jonah rests, was caused to grow by God, giving shade to Jonah and in turn making it a symbol of resurrection and eternal life. Iconographically, *Jonah under the Gourd Vine* evolved from pagan mythological figures who, after sleeping, arose to everlasting life in paradise. The gourd vine, which later spread its shade over the sleeping prophet, clearly prefigured the bliss of paradise. So compelling to the early Christians was the Jonah story that it figured frequently in catacomb painting. The story is commonly found in relief sculpture from sarcophagi, where the entire story is compressed into a single panel. The figure of *Jonah Praying* (fig. 16) with arms extended in the orant position has been interpreted to represent either the moment of Jonah's repentance within the whale's belly or else Jonah giving thanks after his deliverance. The orant position was the position of public prayer in the ancient world. Seen collectively in their original context, the five sculptures would have reinforced these deeply cherished Christian themes. This was the real power of the Jonah Marbles. These four sculptures representing Jonah are the only known freestanding figures of this subject to survive from the early Christian era.

The intended function and original placement of the Jonah Marbles is not definitively known and has been much debated by scholars. Recent studies have argued the possibility that the group may have originally formed a domestic fountain ensemble. Numerous documented examples exist for fountain sculptures in the Roman Empire, both public and domestic, between about 200 and 400 A.D. Although most of these sculptures consist of mythological or idyllic subjects, Christian sculptures are occasionally present as well. In the fourth century, Eusebius, the biographer of Constantine the Great, left a tantalizing description of "fountains in the midst of the market place graced with figures of the Good Shepherd . . . and also that of Daniel in the Lion's Den." If the Cleveland sculptures were meant to adorn a fountain, it would most likely have been within the confines of a private nymphaeum or domestic garden. Encouraged by improvements to the water supply in Rome and in other parts of the Empire, well-to-do citizens began creating elaborate fountain complexes in their villas within which were placed small-scale statues depicting animals, birds, satyrs, Cupid riding a dolphin, and Heracles. The watery subject of the Jonah story would have had particular appeal in this setting. Domestic gardens, besides being centers where families would congregate to take meals, were often the focal point for piety in a variety of forms, both public and private. It is not difficult to imagine the Jonah Marbles in such a context.

It has also been effectively argued that the Jonah ensemble may have derived from a late Roman tomb whose owners were Christian. The biblical story of Jonah held deep significance for early Christians as an allegory of the death and Resurrection of Christ. In this way, it held powerful redemptive implications for the believer. The story of Jonah frequently appeared on the walls and ceilings of the Roman catacombs, and it is possible that the Jonah ensemble may have served a decorative function in the burial chamber of an affluent late Roman Christian family. While their original context and placement are obscure, that they served as potent Christian symbols is beyond doubt.

These marble sculptures were undoubtedly carved for well-to-do Christian inhabitants of the eastern Roman Empire. But what do they tell us stylistically as works of art? They depend in both style and inspiration on antique models, specifically sculpture that we call Hellenistic. Hellenistic civilization was the widespread Greek-tinctured culture that expanded throughout the eastern Mediterranean and Near East in the centuries following the death of Alexander the Great in 323 B.C. Its culture was based in part on ancient Greek ideals of language, literature, and art. The characteristics of Hellenistic sculpture may be seen, for example, in the beard, hair, and tunic of the figure of *Jonah Praying* (see fig. 16), which appears to derive from ancient models of Zeus. The reclining figure of *Jonah under the Gourd Vine* (see fig. 14) recalls Hellenistic depictions of river gods, and the beardless figure of *The Good Shepherd* (see fig. 15) harks back to the face of Alexander himself.

Among Byzantium's many and important contributions to our culture was its role in developing the Greco-Roman heritage of painting the human figure. When western Europe lost the human figure in a maze of animal interlace, Byzantine artists were taking figure painting beyond its classical roles by employing it in daring proportions through mosaics. In the apse of the Church of San Vitale in Ravenna (fig. 17), we confront sixth-century figures of Christ and angels almost twice the size of life. Painting, however, was central in the Byzantine East. Sculpture in the round, the preeminent medium of Greek and Roman art, was abandoned, and large-scale relief sculpture became rare. While the imagery of the ancient gods was largely discarded, in painting a whole new language of imagery was developed to carry a new, deeply Christian worldview.

No phenomenon is more characteristic of Byzantine art than the icon (fig. 18). The icon gives Byzantine art its distinctive formal aesthetic. Moreover, the icon was the genre through which the devices and compositions of antique portraiture were transmitted through the Middle Ages to the Renaissance. Icons were the defining force of Byzantine art.

There exists in the Cleveland Museum of Art one of the earliest icons—the textile *Icon of the Mother of God*—woven in Egypt during the sixth century (see fig. 1). It miraculously survived iconoclasm, or the willful destruction of icons,

Figure 17. *Enthroned Christ
Surrounded by Angels* (detail).
Apse mosaic, ca. 526–47.
Church of San Vitale,
Ravenna. (Photo Credit:
Cameraphoto Arte, Venice/
Art Resource, NY)

the vicissitudes of history, the environment, and the challenges of heat, cold,
and damp. The only other surviving icons from the sixth century are paintings
on wooden panels, largely in the Monastery of Saint Catherine in the Sinai.
The Cleveland tapestry icon is among the earliest icons in the United States.
Its original context remains uncertain. It may have been woven for suspension
over the altar of a church or for use in a private home. The tapestry may have
been portable so that its owner could easily roll it up and carry it. The Cleveland icon speaks with as much power today as in the sixth century.

Icons elicited impassioned responses, both positive and negative. Imperial
policy during the eighth century eventually dictated their destruction. The
debate centered on the appropriate use of icons in religious veneration and

Figure 18. *Icon of Saint Michael the Archangel.* Wood panel. Byzantium, 14th century. Byzantine Museum, Athens. (Photo Credit: Werner Forman/Art Resource, NY)

Figure 19 (facing page, top). *Icon of the Virgin and Child with Archangels and Saints.* Encaustic on wood panel (86.5 x 49.7 x 1.5 cm). Byzantium, Constantinople(?), 6th century. Monastery of Saint Catherine, Mount Sinai, Egypt. (Photo Credit: Erich Lessing/Art Resource, NY)

Figure 20 (facing page, bottom). *Mother of God.* Mosaic, apse concha, 11th century. Church of Hosios Loukas, Greece. (Photo Credit: Erich Lessing/Art Resource, NY)

the precise relationship between the sacred personage and his image. Fear that viewers misdirected their veneration toward the image rather than to the holy person represented in the image lay at the heart of this controversy. Old Testament prohibitions against worshipping graven images (Exodus 20:4) provided one of the most important precedents for Byzantine iconoclasm. The immediate causes for this crisis have been hotly contested by scholars, with some suggesting the rise of Islam was the culprit, while others believe it was the emperor's desire to usurp religious authority and funds.

Iconoclasm literally means "image breaking" and refers to a recurring historical impulse to break, or destroy, images for religious or political reasons.

Within the Byzantine world, iconoclasm refers to a theological debate involving both the Byzantine church and state. The controversy spanned roughly a century, during the years 726–87 and 815–43. In these decades, imperial legislation barred the production and use of figural images; simultaneously, the cross was promoted as the most acceptable decorative form for Byzantine churches. Archaeological evidence suggests that in certain regions of Byzantium, including Constantinople and Nicaea, existing icons were destroyed or plastered over. Very few early Byzantine icons survived the iconoclastic period; notable exceptions were woven icons, painted icons preserved at the Monastery of Saint Catherine on Mount Sinai in Egypt (fig. 19), and the miniature icons found on Byzantine coins, including those of Justinian II (r. 685–95; 705–11). A classic defense of icons was issued by the Second Council of Nicaea, convoked by Empress Irene in 787. It expressed the core tenet in the following terms: "The honor which is paid to the image passes on to that which the image represents, and he who does worship to the image does worship to the person represented in it." Simply put, the icon itself was not being venerated. It served as a vehicle through which the saint or Christ himself was venerated. Popular religious practice favored the veneration of icons, and their use was officially restored and sanctioned in the East under Byzantine emperor Michael III (842–67).[1]

Icons could be monumental, applied directly to the walls of a church. They could also be portable, painted onto panels and hung on walls or sanctuary screens. Icons were made of virtually any material, including ivory, soapstone, and various precious and semiprecious gemstones. Consider the exquisite eleventh-century ivory plaque of the Mother of God in the Cleveland Museum of Art. The solemnity of this ivory is due to its subject matter. The Mother of God was originally the central plaque of a triptych. The Virgin Mary, as she is called in the West, is always referred to as the Mother of God in Orthodox Christian culture. Her image is the most common in Byzantine art and became the standard monumental iconographic theme for the conchae of church apses, especially after the period of iconoclasm (fig. 20).

Though the common perception of icons is of a painting on wood panel, technically refined icons were produced in a variety of media—from textiles

Figure 21. *Cameo of Saint George.* Bloodstone (3.2 x 2.8 cm). Middle Byzantine, Constantinople, 10th–11th century. The Cleveland Museum of Art. Dudley P. Allen Fund 1959.41

to mosaics and ivories. Icons could also have been small enough to fit into a medieval pocket or worn on the neck. A small cameo of Saint George, now in the Cleveland Museum of Art (fig. 21), is exquisitely carved from bloodstone in high relief. Byzantine artists followed the earlier Roman practice of carving precious gemstones and demonstrated considerable skill. Such carved cameos or intaglios were undoubtedly intended for a sophisticated and wealthy elite in Byzantine society. Saint George, along with Saints Demetrios, Theodore, and Prokopios, were some of the military saints popular throughout the Byzantine world. Saint George was considered a powerful protector to the beholder of his likeness. This small cameo bearing his image would have most likely been mounted on a gold frame and worn around the neck. In this way, the owner could have easily touched and kissed it in times of crisis or stress, thus creating a powerful bond between worshipper and saint.

The permanent mural decoration found within the Byzantine church nave followed a special iconographic system that made optimum use of its compact design. The decoration and the architecture complement each other so nicely that the buildings seem made for the images rather than vice versa. The immediacy of this experience is demonstrated the moment the Orthodox enter the church. They begin by circulating to venerate the images of saints, whether in panel icons or mural decoration. The traditional greeting of the icon begins with *proskynesis,* a thrice-repeated deep bow in which one touches the ground with one's right hand and makes the sign of the cross. Next one touches and kisses the icon (the act of which is referred to as *aspasmos*) and lights a candle. Finally, one converses with the saint, addressing one's prayers to the holy figure. Entering the church means entering the communion of saints and joining their ranks (fig. 22).

While these sanctoral icons are located closest to the churchgoer, the great events of the life of Christ are represented higher up, in the vaults surrounding the nave. The narratives, reading from left to right around the nave, picture the same events commemorated by the liturgy, and hence they are called festival icons. In a world where only the educated few were literate, the power of pictorial narrative must have been felt much more forcefully than it is today. But the intent was more than informational; the scenes and images invited the spectator to experience the event represented.

The climax of the nave's artistic program is the larger-than-life image of Christ Pantocrator in the dome (fig. 23). While the proportions of a Byzantine

Figure 22. View of the mosaic of the Hermit Hosios Loukas and vaulted ceiling above seen across an arch. Byzantine, 11th century. Monastery Church, Hosios Loukas, Greece. (Photo Credit: Erich Lessing/Art Resource, NY)

Figure 23. *Dome with Christ Pantocrator and the Four Archangels,* Martorana, Palermo. The church was commissioned in 1143 by George of Antioch, Admiral of Roger II, Norman King of Sicily. The Middle Byzantine mosaics date from ca. 1151. Palermo, Sicily. (Photo Credit: Vanni/ Art Resource, NY)

nave are flexible—some are steeper than others—they are governed by an inscribed isosceles triangle, the apex of which is the summit of the dome and the base of which is the width of the nave. The crown of the dome, therefore, is visible from wherever the viewer stands; that is, the Christ in the dome can see all those he blesses below. This is important in view of the ritual purpose of the nave, for here Christ reads the Gospel book that he holds, enlightening the souls of the believers who receive his ultimate blessing, the sacrament that transforms them into Christ.

The icon had come of age as an art form and occupied the most holy place in the church building. It had also come to occupy a central place in the life of the Byzantines on all levels. On the popular level, miracle stories multiplied around icons; the touch of an icon was thought to have curative powers, and saints were imagined to step out of icons to help people in need. Among the middle class, merchants in Rome were hanging little icons of Saint Symeon Stylites, a Syrian ascetic, over their shops to protect their goods. In 626 the military carried an icon of Christ around the defenses of Constantinople to ward off an assault by the Persians. Emperor Justin II (r. 565–78) placed a mosaic of Christ Enthroned directly over his own throne of the Great Palace, and Justinian II (r. 685–95) put Christ's image on the face of his gold coinage with his own image on the reverse.

The icon was also the subject of serious religious reflection. The reciprocal gaze of the saint seemed especially meaningful. On an icon of the Archangel Michael (see, for example, fig. 18), the poet Agathias (ca. 532–82) remarked: "The mortal man who beholds the image directs his mind to a higher contemplation. His veneration is no longer distracted: engraving within himself the archangel's traits, he trembles as if he were in the latter's presence. The eyes encourage deep thoughts, and art is able by means of colors to ferry over the prayer of the mind."[2] By gazing in the eyes of the icon one could transmit prayers directly to the saint.

The Byzantine Empire existed for just over 1,100 years from its foundation by Constantine in 324 to the fall of Constantinople at the hands of the Ottoman Turks in 1453. During this period, Constantinople was an unwavering beacon of enlightenment and a refuge for the spirit of Greek and Roman antiquity. More than any other cultural force, Byzantium must be credited with

Figure 24. *Icon of the Virgin Hodegetria.* Tempera and gold on wood panel. Master Dionysius, Russian, School of Moscow, 1482. Tretyakov Gallery, Moscow. (Photo Credit: Bildarchiv Preussischer Kulturbesitz/Art Resource, NY)

preserving classical art and culture until the time of its rediscovery during the Renaissance. With the conversion of Vladimir of Kiev in 987, the Slavs of Ukraine and Russia entered into the same Christian Orthodox community as the Byzantines, opening eastern Europe to the culture and artists of Constantinople. After 1453 the Slavic lands of Russia, Ukraine, Serbia, and Bulgaria became the inheritors of Byzantium's religious mantle and of its artistic, cultural, and iconographic traditions. Russian icon painters like Master Dionysius, working in Moscow around 1500, were intellectually and spiritually the continuators of the icon painters of the Monastery of Saint Catherine in the Sinai (fig. 24).

CHAPTER THREE

Images of the Saints, Angels, and Holy Persons

e have already stated that medieval men and women were seemingly more emotional than their modern counterparts. In the collections of the Cleveland Museum of Art is a fourteenth-century sculpture in polychromed wood of *Christ and Saint John the Evangelist* (fig. 25). The sculpture originated in southern Germany in the region of the Bodensee, Lake Constance, and indeed this subject is found mainly within this region. It is conceivable that the sculpture was produced for one of the many monasteries or convents around Lake Constance. Though smaller versions of this sculpture are known to have adorned the cells of nuns as a visual focus for their devotions, the size of the Cleveland sculpture suggests that it would have been placed on a subsidiary altar in a small side chapel of the conventual church.[1] It would have served there as a votive object during communal prayer. On other occasions, such as on special feast days, the sculpture may have been carried in ritual procession through the church or even through the streets of a nearby town. The Cleveland *Christ and Saint John* is in many ways an exemplar of the emotive role of religious art during the Middle Ages. Saint John is depicted as the disciple "whom Jesus loved," who reclined on Jesus's bosom at the Last Supper (John 13:23). It was at the Last Supper when Jesus announced to the disciples that one of them would betray him. At this, John immediately cast himself on Jesus's bosom weeping.

Figure 25. *Christ and Saint John the Evangelist*. Polychromed and gilded wood (H. 92.7 cm). Germany, Swabia (near Lake Constance), early 14th century. The Cleveland Museum of Art. Purchase from the J. H. Wade Fund 1928.753

This emotionally charged moment has been isolated by the sculptor and turned into an object inspiring prayer and meditation. Jesus is shown tenderly taking the hand of John with his right hand, while placing his left arm over the disciple's shoulder to offer comfort. This image would have invoked great passion, devotion, and unspeakable emotion. Figural groups representing Saint John resting on the Bosom of Christ were localized in their popularity and distribution. Such groups were commonly found within the convents of Swabia in southwestern Germany, particularly near Lake Constance. The appeal of such imagery to a feminine audience may be accounted for by biblical commentaries and sermons of the period in which John is often identified as the bridegroom of the marriage of Cana and the bride of the Song of Songs.

This imagery with its bridal overtones presented the evangelist as the ideal model for feminine self-identification and mysticism, strongly alluding to the union of the soul with God. It is perhaps difficult for the modern viewer of this sculpture to perceive it as the centerpiece of mystical contemplation and a source of emotive energy, as it was in its original context and setting.

The exaltation of art and artists has been a common feature of Western society for the past five hundred years, that is to say, since the Renaissance. There is little evidence, however, that this sort of thinking was anything but alien to the people of the Middle Ages. Presumably those who passed through any

Figure 26. *Pórtico de la Gloria*. Central portal and entrance to the nave. Work of Master Mateo, 1168–1188. Cathedral of Santiago de Compostela (Galicia), Spain. (Photo Credit: Scala/Art Resource, NY)

form of academic training were instilled with certain prejudices toward the visual arts. Painting, sculpture, and building were viewed as the "mechanical arts," and artists were simple "artificers," or craftsmen. This prejudice, traceable back to Aristotle, was embraced by the Christian church, which placed contemplation above action. Material things, such as paintings and sculptures, were only of value for their capacity to reveal certain aspects of the heavenly realm and the mysteries of God. Medieval iconography developed through the symbiotic relationship of artist and cleric. The great sculptural programs of European churches were probably laid out by a cleric, perhaps a canon of a cathedral or an abbot or possibly a committee of clerics (fig. 26). It was incumbent on the artist to know the rules and to deliver the "script" as written. Medieval scholars valued order and codification. They organized art along set principles in much the same way they organized religious dogma, education, and society itself.

Any artist practicing his craft was expected to know these principles. He would know, for example, that a halo placed behind the head of a person signified sanctity, but a cruciform halo, one inscribed with a cross at center, signified divinity (fig. 27). A cruciform halo was only used in conjunction with the three

Figure 27. *Painted Crucifix* (Detail of Christ's head and halo). Tempera and oil with gold on wood (186.63 x 160.65 cm). Italy, Pisa, ca. 1230–1240. The Cleveland Museum of Art. Leonard C. Hanna Jr. Fund 1995.5

Figure 28 (left). *Tympanum with Christ in Majesty, Royal Portal*, ca. 1145–1155. Cathedral, Chartres, France. (Photo Credit: Scala/Art Resource, NY)

Figure 29 (below). *Enthroned Virgin and Child*. Oak with linen, gesso, and polychromy (H. 76.8 cm). France, Auvergne, late 12th century. The Metropolitan Museum of Art. Gift of J. Pierpont Morgan Acc. 16.32.194. (Photo credit: Image copyright © The Metropolitan Museum of Art/Art Resource, NY)

persons of the Trinity. Indeed, God the Father, Christ, and the Holy Spirit were never permitted to be represented in art without the cruciform halo. One of the most common images encountered in medieval art, particularly in church portal sculpture, is Christ as the all-sovereign Ruler of the World, the *Pantocrator*. A particularly fine example is in the tympanum of the central portal of the west facade at Chartres Cathedral (fig. 28). Christ, with the cruciform halo behind his head, is shown seated and enthroned, raising his right hand in blessing while holding the book of Gospels in his left. His entire body is placed within an almond-shaped surround, a kind of body halo, called an aureole, which suggested eternal bliss. The sculptor would have been required to know that the aureole, expressing eternal beatitude, belonged exclusively to the three persons of the Trinity, the Virgin, and the souls of the blessed.

An artist would have also been required to know that it was forbidden to cover the feet of Christ; they had to be shown uncovered. However, the feet

Figure 30. *Miniature: Christ as Judge of the World.* Tempera and gold on parchment (21.3 x 18.2 cm). Germany, Regensburg, ca. 1330. The Cleveland Museum of Art. Purchase from the J. H. Wade Fund 1953.637

of his mother, the Virgin Mary, were required to be covered, never bare (fig. 29). Most likely, this stricture had the same significance as the requirement that the Virgin always be represented in a veil, probably a visual reminder of her purity and Virgin birth. Interestingly, the saints, with the exception of the apostles, are also shown with covered feet; like Christ, the apostles are depicted with bare feet. In other words, an artist needed to be aware that bare feet were a sign by which God, the angels, Christ, and the apostles could be recognized visually in art.

In scenes representing the Last Judgment, Christ is often depicted with other visual elements. A fourteenth-century German miniature of the subject reveals Christ, the final judge, seated on a throne in the form of a tricolored rainbow (fig. 30). The rainbow's three colors symbolize the Trinity. Two swords emanate from his mouth—the Swords of Justice—which visually reinforce the role of Christ as the last judge. To complete the scene, two trumpet-blowing angels announce the final moment as the dead arise from their graves.

A Dutch version of the same subject appears within the pages of a mid-fifteenth-century book of hours, a private prayer book for the layperson. It again shows Christ seated on a rainbow, once again with the Sword of Justice and angels trumpeting, but here the scene is more graphic (fig. 31). Before the gates of what appears to be a town or city, a lone figure stands holding a key. This, of course, can only be Saint Peter standing before the gates of heaven. Once again, the viewer is shown the dead rising from their graves. Opposite Peter is a great monster with a gaping mouth—the "Mouth of Hell"—within which may be seen the souls of the damned amid the eternal flames. Such images provided graphic lessons to the lay owners of these private prayer books, or books of hours.

The texts of a book of hours consisted of a cycle of prayers, psalms, antiphons, hymns, and other devotional material arranged around the eight liturgical hours of the day, otherwise known as the Office of the Virgin Mary. These devotions were modeled after the offices for the canonical hours practiced in monastic communities. This series of daily devotions, known as the Divine Office, would be recited starting at Matins, around 2:30 A.M., and finally finishing with Compline in the evening. Although the laity probably did not adhere completely to this rigorous schedule for their private devotions, their books were divided into the same eight parts, hence the name "book of hours." Their direct inspiration was, therefore, the breviary, a manuscript made exclusively for the use of the clergy and members of religious orders. While the owner

Figure 31. *The Last Judgment.* Fol. 157v. from a *Book of Hours,* ca. 1460–1465. Ink, tempera, and gold on vellum (15.9 x 11.6 cm). Master of Gijsbrecht van Brederode, Dutch, Utrecht, active ca. 1455–1475. The Cleveland Museum of Art. Gift of Milton B. Freudenheim in memory of his wife, Elizabeth Ege Freudenheim, 1998.124

and Jacob de Voragine's *Legenda aurea* interpreted the chronology of human history, not by the lives of kings and emperors, but by those of the saints. The saints—apostles, doctors, virgins, and martyrs—whether simple shepherdesses or learned bishops, were seen, because of their virtuous lives, as the true heroes of human history. They were therefore appropriate intercessors, models, and patrons for living Christians. Major saints were venerated widely across Europe, whereas many lesser-known local saints were venerated only in a particular diocese, region, or town. For example, only in the Flemish towns of Ghent and Bruges was Saint Bavo known and venerated. In the French town of Rouen it was Saint Donation, while in Paris, Saint Geneviève was exclusively venerated. Only in England were Saints Edmund and Edward the Confessor venerated. Some saints thus had special significance for particular regions or dioceses, but outside of these areas they may have not been well known. The challenge for the medieval church and, by extension, for medieval artists was to devise cogent ways to visually reveal individual saints to the faithful so that their identities could not be confused.

Artists were required to follow these officially sanctioned conventions. They were expected to know, for example, that Saint Paul was always represented with a long dark beard and a slightly bald pate. He holds a sword as his attribute, the instrument of his martyrdom—he was beheaded outside the gates of Rome. Saint Peter, however, was always depicted as an older man with a short, round beard and full head of short, curly hair, either gray or white (fig. 33).

Figure 33. *Saints Peter and Paul.* Two fresco fragments from Old St. Peter's Basilica in Rome, ca. 1250–1300. Vatican Museums, Vatican City. (Photo Credit: Saskia Ltd./Art Resource, NY)

Figure 34. *Saint John the Evangelist.* Fol. 171v. from *The Hours of Queen Isabella the Catholic of Spain,* ca. 1497–1500. Ink, tempera, and gold on vellum (22.5 x 15.2 cm). Alexander Bening and Associates, Flemish, Ghent, active ca. 1470–1519. The Cleveland Museum of Art. Purchase, Leonard C. Hanna Jr. Bequest 1963.256

Peter customarily holds a key or keys as his attribute, the keys to the kingdom of heaven granted to him by Jesus. In art, Peter and Paul are often shown together as they share the same feast day (June 29). Due to these established artistic conventions, each of the two saints was never confused with the other.

Similarly, Saint John the Evangelist is often represented in art holding a chalice (fig. 34). After the death of Christ, the apostle was challenged by the pagan priest of the Temple of Diana to drink from a poison chalice to illustrate the sincerity of his faith. John consumed the poison potion and survived. Occasionally artists depict a snake or small dragon emerging from the chalice as a symbolic representation of Satan.

Quite often the identification of a saint depends on a particular event or incident in the life of that saint. The *Miracle of Saint Anthony of Padua*, for example, was an important image in Franciscan devotions (fig. 35). Here the

Figure 35. *Miracle of Saint Anthony of Padua*. Fol. 187v. from *The Hours of Queen Isabella the Catholic of Spain*, ca. 1497–1500. Ink, tempera, and gold on vellum (22.5 x 15.2 cm). Alexander Bening and Associates, Flemish, Ghent, active ca. 1470–1519. The Cleveland Museum of Art. Purchase, Leonard C. Hanna Jr. Bequest 1963.256

Figure 36. *Saint Jerome with the Lion*. Alabaster with traces of polychromy (37.8 x 28.1 x 15.9 cm), ca. 1490–1495. Tilman Riemenschneider, German, Würzburg, ca. 1460–1531. The Cleveland Museum of Art. Purchase from the J. H. Wade Fund 1946.82

saint, clad in Franciscan garb, suspends the host before a mule, which kneels in homage. The crowd of nonbelievers is thus convinced of the truth of the mystery of transubstantiation. Similarly, Saint Jerome, one of the Four Fathers of the church, is commonly identified by his attribute, a lion (fig. 36). Jerome was the abbot of a monastery. His legend holds that a lion injured with a thorn in its paw entered the saint's monastery. The other monks ran away in fear, but Jerome in an act of kindness embraced the lion and removed the thorn. Afterward, the lion became his devoted companion. Saint Jerome is also recognized in art by his cardinal's hat.

Saint Roch (or Rocco in Italian) was remembered in Christian hagiographies as a man of compassion and charity (fig. 37). He was known to feed and minister to victims of the plague. When Roch contracted the plague himself, he was ostracized and forbidden to mingle with the townspeople. Because Roch was unable to obtain food, God sent him a small dog who brought him a loaf of bread each day. Thus, Saint Roch is often depicted revealing his plague sore to an attending angel. He is typically accompanied by a small dog, which

Figure 37. *Saint Roch.* Fol. 181v. from *The Hours of Queen Isabella the Catholic of Spain,* ca. 1497–1500. Ink, tempera, and gold on vellum (22.5 x 15.2 cm). Gerard Horenbout, Flemish, Ghent. The Cleveland Museum of Art. Purchase, Leonard C. Hanna Jr. Bequest 1963.256

holds a loaf of bread in its mouth. Saint Roch was well known throughout Europe during the Middle Ages.

Another saint identifiable through a singular act of charity was Saint Martin of Tours (see fig. 32). Martin, a Roman centurion known for his compassion, was an early saint of the church. While riding his horse, Martin encountered a poor beggar who was naked, cold, and shivering. Martin removed his own cloak, cut it in half with his sword, and gave half of it to the beggar. The saint is typically identified by this incident, emblematic of his charity, and is shown in painting and sculpture in the act of dividing his cloak with a sword. Saint Martin eventually became the Bishop of Tours in central France.

Saint Margaret is represented by a superb sculpture in the Cleveland Museum of Art attributed to the Sicilian sculptor Antonello Gaggini (fig. 38) and originally made for Palermo Cathedral. Antonello Gagini, a member of a large family of sculptors, had a workshop in Palermo and supplied monumental religious sculptures to the cathedrals of Palermo, Messina, and Montelione in Calabria. After 1507, Antonello himself worked for fifteen years producing marble sculptures for Palermo Cathedral. Though its exact provenance is unknown, this figure of the legendary virgin martyr Saint Margaret was most likely commissioned for one of these ecclesiastical foundations, possibly the chancel of Palermo Cathedral. According to legend, Margaret, wishing to remain a Christian virgin, refused to marry the pagan Olybrius, the prefect of Antioch. As punishment, she was cruelly tortured and thrown into a dungeon. There, Satan appeared to her in the form of a dragon and attempted to swallow her. However, the devout saint held a cross in her hand that scorched the monster's throat, forcing it to disgorge her. Margaret miraculously emerged unharmed. This sensitively carved sculpture shows Margaret reading from her book of hours, a sign of her piety, as she tramples on a dragon. The dragon became the saint's attribute in sacred art by which she is recognized. Margaret was, finally, beheaded after praying that women in labor who invoked her might safely deliver their child, just as she was safely delivered from the dragon's belly. Margaret's great popularity derived from her patronage of women in childbirth. She was widely venerated in southern Europe throughout the sixteenth and seventeenth centuries after which time her popularity began to decline. Ecclesiastical authorities removed Margaret from the church calendar in 1969 since there was little evidence that her story, while inspiring, was anything more than a legend.

Such stories abound in medieval hagiographies and were extremely popular throughout the later Middle Ages. Artists adapted elements from these stories to give the saints a visual and material presence—all through the vehicle of art.

Figure 38. *Saint Margaret.* Marble (H. 139.7 cm), ca. 1520–1530. Antonello Gaggini, Italian, Sicily, Palermo, 1478–1536. The Cleveland Museum of Art. Purchase from the J. H. Wade Fund 1942.564

While some deviation occurs, the images are surprisingly consistent in their portrayal of the saints. A common saintly attribute found in medieval art is the palm branch. When held by a saint, it signifies martyrdom. Instruments of martyrdom are also commonly seen: Saint Catherine of Alexandria with her wheel, Saint Stephen with the stones (fig. 39), and Saint Lawrence with the grill (fig. 40). Such elements helped the pious quickly identify a particular saint, whether they encountered one through art for public worship in an ecclesiastical context or one produced for the private devotion of a single patron and used in a domestic setting.

In addition to the saints, angels were ubiquitous figures in the artistic traditions of medieval and Renaissance Europe. Angels were not human but celestial entities created by God to serve his will, principally as messengers between himself and humankind, but also as agents to enforce that will on earth. Another function of angels was to praise and adore God. While this was also expected of men, angels were in the continuous presence of God and thus, unlike man, beholding the beatific vision. Like humankind, angels are created beings, though generally accepted as beings higher than man in rank. "You have made him [man] a little less than the angels" (Psalms 8:4). In traditional Christian iconography, angels are regarded as being asexual and belonging

Figure 39 (left). *Saint Stephen.* Lindenwood with polychromy (H. 93.5 cm), ca. 1508. Tilman Riemenschneider, German, Würzburg, ca. 1460–1531. The Cleveland Museum of Art. Leonard C. Hanna Jr. Fund 1959.43

Figure 40 (right). *Saint Lawrence.* Lindenwood with polychromy (H. 93.5 cm), ca. 1502. Tilman Riemenschneider, German, Würzburg, ca. 1460–1531. The Cleveland Museum of Art. Leonard C. Hanna Jr. Fund 1959.42

holds a loaf of bread in its mouth. Saint Roch was well known throughout Europe during the Middle Ages.

Another saint identifiable through a singular act of charity was Saint Martin of Tours (see fig. 32). Martin, a Roman centurion known for his compassion, was an early saint of the church. While riding his horse, Martin encountered a poor beggar who was naked, cold, and shivering. Martin removed his own cloak, cut it in half with his sword, and gave half of it to the beggar. The saint is typically identified by this incident, emblematic of his charity, and is shown in painting and sculpture in the act of dividing his cloak with a sword. Saint Martin eventually became the Bishop of Tours in central France.

Saint Margaret is represented by a superb sculpture in the Cleveland Museum of Art attributed to the Sicilian sculptor Antonello Gaggini (fig. 38) and originally made for Palermo Cathedral. Antonello Gagini, a member of a large family of sculptors, had a workshop in Palermo and supplied monumental religious sculptures to the cathedrals of Palermo, Messina, and Montelione in Calabria. After 1507, Antonello himself worked for fifteen years producing marble sculptures for Palermo Cathedral. Though its exact provenance is unknown, this figure of the legendary virgin martyr Saint Margaret was most likely commissioned for one of these ecclesiastical foundations, possibly the chancel of Palermo Cathedral. According to legend, Margaret, wishing to remain a Christian virgin, refused to marry the pagan Olybrius, the prefect of Antioch. As punishment, she was cruelly tortured and thrown into a dungeon. There, Satan appeared to her in the form of a dragon and attempted to swallow her. However, the devout saint held a cross in her hand that scorched the monster's throat, forcing it to disgorge her. Margaret miraculously emerged unharmed. This sensitively carved sculpture shows Margaret reading from her book of hours, a sign of her piety, as she tramples on a dragon. The dragon became the saint's attribute in sacred art by which she is recognized. Margaret was, finally, beheaded after praying that women in labor who invoked her might safely deliver their child, just as she was safely delivered from the dragon's belly. Margaret's great popularity derived from her patronage of women in childbirth. She was widely venerated in southern Europe throughout the sixteenth and seventeenth centuries after which time her popularity began to decline. Ecclesiastical authorities removed Margaret from the church calendar in 1969 since there was little evidence that her story, while inspiring, was anything more than a legend.

Such stories abound in medieval hagiographies and were extremely popular throughout the later Middle Ages. Artists adapted elements from these stories to give the saints a visual and material presence—all through the vehicle of art.

Figure 38. *Saint Margaret.* Marble (H. 139.7 cm), ca. 1520–1530. Antonello Gaggini, Italian, Sicily, Palermo, 1478–1536. The Cleveland Museum of Art. Purchase from the J. H. Wade Fund 1942.564

While some deviation occurs, the images are surprisingly consistent in their portrayal of the saints. A common saintly attribute found in medieval art is the palm branch. When held by a saint, it signifies martyrdom. Instruments of martyrdom are also commonly seen: Saint Catherine of Alexandria with her wheel, Saint Stephen with the stones (fig. 39), and Saint Lawrence with the grill (fig. 40). Such elements helped the pious quickly identify a particular saint, whether they encountered one through art for public worship in an ecclesiastical context or one produced for the private devotion of a single patron and used in a domestic setting.

In addition to the saints, angels were ubiquitous figures in the artistic traditions of medieval and Renaissance Europe. Angels were not human but celestial entities created by God to serve his will, principally as messengers between himself and humankind, but also as agents to enforce that will on earth. Another function of angels was to praise and adore God. While this was also expected of men, angels were in the continuous presence of God and thus, unlike man, beholding the beatific vision. Like humankind, angels are created beings, though generally accepted as beings higher than man in rank. "You have made him [man] a little less than the angels" (Psalms 8:4). In traditional Christian iconography, angels are regarded as being asexual and belonging

Figure 39 (left). *Saint Stephen.* Lindenwood with polychromy (H. 93.5 cm), ca. 1508. Tilman Riemenschneider, German, Würzburg, ca. 1460–1531. The Cleveland Museum of Art. Leonard C. Hanna Jr. Fund 1959.43

Figure 40 (right). *Saint Lawrence.* Lindenwood with polychromy (H. 93.5 cm), ca. 1502. Tilman Riemenschneider, German, Würzburg, ca. 1460–1531. The Cleveland Museum of Art. Leonard C. Hanna Jr. Fund 1959.42

to neither gender. Angels are present in many of the major narrative events in religious art, such as the Annunciation to the Virgin and the Shepherds, the Flight into Egypt, the Nativity, the Resurrection, and others. Angels are often shown accompanying the souls of the elect aloft toward heaven, and their presence, pictorially speaking, signifies divine blessing or approval. They occur in both Old and New Testament contexts. In the former, they are referenced as protectors of the righteous (Abraham) and punishers of evil doers (Genesis 19: the destruction of Sodom and Gomorrah). Indeed, the Christian concept of angels appears to have derived from Jewish prototypes. They are not unique to Judaism or Christianity, though, and appear even earlier in the traditions of the ancient Near East. Four- and six-winged angels, often with only their face and wings showing, drawn from the higher grades of angels, especially cherubim and seraphim, are derived from Persian art and are usually shown only in heaven, not on earth. They often appear in the pendentives of domes or semidomes of churches. It might be noted that in the Greek and Roman pantheon, Mercury appears as the winged messenger of Jupiter. Medieval Christianity, however, embraced the concept of angels with deep fervor, and their presence in prophetic and apocalyptic literature had a deep and abiding impact on forming an involved angelic iconography.

The earliest known Christian image of an angel dates to the mid-third century and is found in the *Cubicolo dell'Annunziazione* in the Catacomb of Priscilla. It is depicted without wings. Similar wingless representations of angels appear on early sarcophagi and small objects such as lamps and reliquaries. The earliest known figurative representation of an angel with wings appears on a sarcophagus frontal in Constantinople dating to the reign of Theodosius I (379–95). Apart from these early exceptions, Christian art throughout the Middle Ages represented angels consistently with wings from the fourth century forward. By the fifth century, the early church developed a system of categorizing angels into nine choirs, or three heirarchies, each with a specific mission. These are (from highest to lowest rank):

CHOIR	FUNCTION
Seraphim	
Cherubim	Perpetual adoration of God
Thrones	
Dominations	
Virtues	Governance of the stars and the elements
Powers	
Princedoms	
Archangels	Divine messengers
Angels	

Figure 41. *Miniature from a Gradual: Initial G[audeamus omnes in Domino]*. Ink, tempera, and gold on vellum (38.6 x 36.5 cm), ca. 1371–77. Don Silvestro dei Gherarducci. Italian, Florence, 1339–99. The Cleveland Museum of Art. Purchase from the J. H. Wade Fund 1930.105

Such heirarchies of angels presented artists with a conceptual framework to support their representation of the heavenly realm. Seraphim and cherubim are normally depicted with heads only (no bodies) and with one, two, or three pair of wings. The seraph is typically painted red, and the cherub blue (sometimes golden yellow). These two categories are frequently used in conjunction with God the Father, Christ in Majesty, the Coronation of the Virgin, the Last Judgment, and other themes that are explored visually within a celestial or heavenly context.

An example of this is found in a Florentine illuminated initial G, dating to about 1371, and now in the Cleveland Museum of Art (fig. 41). This initial, excised from a manuscript gradual, would have introduced the text *Gaudeamus omnes in Domino* (Let us rejoice in the Lord), which is the beginning of Introit for the Feast of All Saints (November 1). The highly chromatic initial with punched and burnished gold represents the enthroned godhead Christ (King of Justice), with his mother, the Virgin Mary (Queen of Mercy), seated at his right. Rows of saints and angels turn toward them in adoration. Christ and the Virgin hold scepters as symbols of their sovereignty and sit on a throne surrounded by vividly painted seraphim and cherubim. These are shown closest to the godhead. The setting is a flowery meadow symbolizing the peace and tranquility of the heavenly realm. Below, music-making angels of the lower hierarchy intensify the composition, and around the enthroned Christ and Virgin is the heavenly court of All Saints. Here, the artist has brilliantly painted each—apostles, deacons, Old Testament heroes, church fathers, hermit saints, and virgins—with individuality and distinct characterizations. The result is a magnificent composition rivaling those of the Trecento altarpiece. It is a masterpiece of Renaissance manuscript painting.

This monumental initial G, along with other dispersed fragments, has long been known to derive from a large set of choral books produced in the Camaldolese monastery of Santa Maria degli Angeli in Florence. The Cleveland miniature appeared on the verso of folio 155 in Corale 2 (now Medicea Laurenziana Library, Florence). The output of the scriptorium of Santa Maria degli Angeli is known to have been extensive. Throughout the second half of the fourteenth century, it produced liturgical books not only for its own use but also for the nearby hospital of Santa Maria Nuova. The decoration of these splendid choral books has traditionally been attributed to Don Silvestro dei Gherarducci, a monk who entered the monastery in 1348 at the age of nine and died there in 1399. Gherarducci was mentioned by Vasari for the excellence of his manuscript painting. It appears that he spent time in Siena learning his craft. Numerous illuminations from liturgical manuscripts as well as some small panels have been attributed to his hand.

The Feast of All Saints, as depicted in the Cleveland miniature, was established in 835 and was inspired by a source in the Book of Revelation (5:11, 7:9) for its iconography:

> Then as I looked I heard the voices of countless angels. These were all around the throne . . . and they cried out aloud: Worthy is the Lamb, and the Lamb that was slain. . . . After this I looked and saw a vast throng, which no one could count, from every nation, of all tribes, peoples, and languages, standing in front of the throne and before the Lamb.

57362

Figure 42. *The Annunciation.* Oil on panel (75.2 x 69.0 cm). Albrecht Bouts, Netherlandish, ca. 1452–1549. The Cleveland Museum of Art. John L. Severance Collection 1942.635

Artists may not have represented the remaining choirs of angels with distinctive attributes or colors, but they usually have human bodies. The powers and other lower orders of angels were sometimes depicted in armor. Most prominent among these is Michael, who is distinguished as both angel and saint. Angels, especially the Archangel Michael (see fig. 18), who were depicted as military-style agents of God, were shown wearing Late Antique military uniform. This could be either the normal military dress—with a knee-length tunic, armor breastplate, and pteruges—or the specific dress of the bodyguard of the Byzantine emperor, which was a long tunic and the loros, a long gold and jewelled pallium restricted to the imperial family and their closest guards. In the West, the basic military dress was still shown in pictures into the Baroque period and beyond, and up to the present day in Eastern Orthodox icons. Other angels, especially Gabriel in Annunciation scenes, were conventionally depicted in long robes, and in the later Middle Ages they often wore the vestments of a deacon—a cope over a dalmatic—as in the Annunciation by Albrecht Bouts (fig. 42).

While Christ, the Virgin, and the saints were represented realistically by artists, symbolism continued to play an important role in the Christian art of the later Middle Ages. As indicated previously, the early Christians had embraced a vocabulary of such symbols as the palm (victory over death) and the lamb (Christ). Throughout the later medieval period, other symbols continued to abound. Most notable are the symbols used for the Four Evangelists, Saints

Figure 43. *Christ in Majesty surrounded by Evangelist Symbols.* Fol. 64 recto from *The Gotha Missal.* Ink, tempera, and gold on vellum (27.1 x 19.5 cm). France, Paris, ca. 1375. The Cleveland Museum of Art. Mr. and Mrs. William H. Marlatt Fund 1962.287

Figure 44. *Christ Pantocrator.* Byzantine mosaic, ca. 1150. Duomo, Cefalu, Sicily. (Photo Credit: Scala/Art Resource, NY)

Matthew, Mark, Luke, and John. Their symbols were the winged man (Matthew), the lion (Mark), the ox (Luke), and the eagle (John). These symbols derive from the vision of the prophet Ezekiel in which he beheld God enthroned among four creatures that had the faces of a man, lion, ox, and eagle, each with four wings (fig. 43). These "apocalyptic beasts" recur in the Book of Revelation but are commonly seen in representations of Christ in Majesty, as in *The Gotha Missal,* a fourteenth-century French illuminated manuscript now in the Cleveland Museum of Art. When the triumphal Christ raises his hand to bless, he uses two fingers. These symbolize his dual nature, human and divine (fig. 44). His remaining three fingers, which touch, represent the three persons of the Trinity. In this sacred artistic script, symbolism as well as placement, arrangement, symmetry, number, and color all have their role. The hierarchy of the blessed in heaven was respected in artistic media, just as there existed on earth a ranking of men and women based on social condition.[4] A higher place in an artistic composition implied honor, superior dignity, and rank, as did a position on the proper right side of Christ. Such a classification is often seen in the Judgment portals of medieval cathedrals in which the Church Triumphant shows successively the orders of patriarchs, prophets, apostles, confessors, martyrs, virgins, and others. And indeed, this system of classification is reflected in the church's Litany of the Saints, an ancient incantation extending back to the earliest Christian liturgy.[5]

Similarly, the use of color in art was used to convey a host of symbolic meanings. Black was a symbol of death and by extension suggested mourning, sickness, or negation. Liturgically, black was the color for Good Friday. Blue symbolized heaven and heavenly love. It was also the symbolic color of truth, since blue always appears in the sky after the clouds are dispelled, suggesting the unveiling of truth. Blue was also the traditional color of the Virgin Mary. Pictorially, she was nearly always represented in a blue mantle in Western art, especially when holding the Christ Child or otherwise shown with him, and particularly in scenes representing the Annunciation (see fig. 42). Brown symbolized the renunciation of the world, hence the color adopted by Franciscan friars and capuchin monks. Purple has always symbolized royal or imperial power. As such, it was often used as a symbol of God the Father and was widely used in Byzantine art for representations of Christ and the Virgin. Also the color of sorrow and penitence, purple was thus used liturgically during Advent and Lent, the church's seasons for preparation and penitence. White, the symbol of innocence, purity, and holiness, was worn by Christ after his Resurrection and also by the Virgin Mary to represent her Immaculate Conception. These and other colors held various grades of meaning and could be exploited in painting, manuscript illumination, stained glass, and painted sculpture to convey basic Christian concepts or the subtleties of moral precepts. Every artist of the Middle Ages who undertook commissions for the production of religious art—and very often, secular art—was required to understand the palette of symbolic meaning. Grave errors would result in the loss of work, ecclesiastical reprimand, or, at worst, accusations of religious heresy.[6]

CHAPTER FOUR

Mater Gloriosa

The Cult of Mary in the Middle Ages

The Virgin Mary, the Madonna, the mother of Jesus is perhaps the most ubiquitous of all sacred images in Christendom, East or West, save perhaps that of the Crucified Christ. In Orthodox Christianity she is customarily never referred to as the Virgin, by which she is commonly known in the West, but simply as the Mother of God—Theotokos, the God bearer in Greek (see fig. 20). From the very early centuries of Christianity, she has held a unique position as intercessor with her son on behalf of sinners. As such, she is accorded particular honor, more so than the saints. While God is owed adoration and the saints veneration, Mary occupies the principal mediating position as an entity belonging to both earth and heaven. Both the Orthodox and Latin Churches accord her particular honor, over and above that due the saints.

As such, her appeal was considerable to those who commissioned her likeness and to those artists who portrayed her during the Middle Ages—a period that defined the way in which she was perceived and represented. The little information we have about Mary is contained in the Gospels of the Four Evangelists. Popularized during the second century as Christianity developed, these accounts say nothing of her face or appearance but simply record episodes in her life, such as the Annunciation (see fig. 42) and the Visitation, specific incidents in the childhood of Jesus in which she played a part; also noted is her presence at the Passion. Her wonderfully rich iconography owes only a small part to the Gospels. It seems to have evolved over the centuries out of a need of the church for a mother figure and a grassroots interest in details of her life. While we cannot know what she looked like, presumably she was no different from any other young woman of first-century Judea. Generations of artists have speculated about her features based on European prototypes. From the apocryphal Gospels and from oral tradition, we learn other details concerning her life—for example, the Virgin went to live with Saint John in Ephesus, where she died ten or twelve years after the death of Jesus in 40 or 42 A.D.

In the first centuries of Christianity, we find no visual representations of Christ, his mother, or the apostles. The Jewish tradition permitted no such images. Not until the second or third century did the first mosaics and murals appear in which Christ and the Virgin were depicted. These were the early icons. At that time, the Virgin appeared in the Christian art found in the catacombs as a veiled woman with her hands raised in prayer, a type known as the *Virgin Orans* (fig. 45). Early mosaics also depicted her as a queen, crowned like a Byzantine empress.

In the calendar of the Orthodox Church, no fewer than five of the twelve great feasts honor her. In Byzantine art, therefore, the Virgin's image dominates as the subject for icons. Many of these depict her in various poses, usually holding the Christ Child. The most famous of these based on its pedigree,

Figure 45. *Virgin Orans and Christ Child.* Catacomb fresco in lunette. Early Christian. Catacomb of the Cimitero Maggiore, Rome. (Photo Credit: Scala/Art Resource, NY)

supposedly drawn from life, is the *Virgin Hodegetria* (see fig. 24). Tradition holds that Saint Luke painted a half-length portrait of the Virgin holding the child on the mountain of Jerusalem. Popular accounts relate how this original portrait was gifted to and acquired by various prominent patrons. A popular legend states that Eudokia, wife of Emperor Theodosios II (r. 408–50), acquired the portrait when she made a pilgrimage to the Holy Land in 438. It was eventually accepted as the portrait from life made by Luke. It received the designation Hodegetria ("she who points the way"), perhaps from the Monastery of the Hodegon in which it was once housed. Tradition holds that the original painting was destroyed by the Turks when Constantinople was captured in 1453. However, numerous copies of the original prototype were produced and continue to be produced. Installed in churches across Orthodox Christianity, these icons became objects of veneration and stimulated the growth and expansion of the Marian cult.

The image of the Virgin Mary, formed and animated by different people for different reasons, is a truly popular creation. She is the protagonist in the drama of the incarnation and the redemption of mankind by Christ and, consequently, in the personal salvation of every individual. As an ordinary woman who gave birth to Christ and in whom all new life is found, Mary became the symbolic mother of the Christian Church. She represents one of the few female figures to have attained the status of myth—a myth that for nearly two thousand years has coursed deeply through Western culture. The ubiquitous image of the Virgin and Child has become the idyllic subject par excellence of medieval art. Implicit to her iconography are multiple and complex questions concerning the Marian image—its symbolic power, emotive force, and central position in the Christian ethos.

From the seventh century, it was customary to represent the Virgin wearing a dark blue mantle and veil (see fig. 1). Blue was the color of heaven and white the color of purity. These colors were consistently associated with her in both the Latin and Orthodox traditions. The theological ideas that the Virgin stood for gradually became more and more inaccessible to artists. By the middle of the fourteenth century, the image of the mother and child had lost the solemnity of earlier art. It had become merely human and intimate, now increasingly removed from the solemn force and beauty of the "Virgin Queen" of the twelfth and thirteenth centuries. From the solemn figure represented on church portals of the thirteenth century, the Virgin became a reflection of everywoman as she was depicted in the intimate and domestic interiors of northern panel painting during the fifteenth and early sixteenth centuries.

Throughout the Middle Ages, the aristocracy opened its purses to build churches in the Virgin's honor, to commission paintings, statues, masses, and votive crowns for her shrines. Starting in the twelfth century, however, the Virgin became the focus of a vigorous and fertile grassroots piety. Through apocryphal stories and legends, the narrative of the Virgin's life and death developed into a myth of epic proportion. For many centuries the Virgin has inspired thousands of artists who labored innumerable hours creating her images in different styles, materials, and techniques. Her image is found in virtually all media, including painting in its many forms (panel, fresco, manuscript painting), mosaics, sculpture, textile, and all sorts of diminutive objects intended for personal devotion, such as ivories, metalwork, and enamels. Images of the Virgin during the Middle Ages essentially fall into four categories: (1) the Virgin alone, (2) the Virgin and Child, (3) the Virgin with other figures, and (4) narrative scenes taken from the life of the Virgin. Each of these broad categories, or genres, has multiple variations replete with its own symbolism.

In the first category, the Virgin was typically represented standing in glory and surrounded by an aureole, or she was depicted enthroned. Such types when appearing in the West probably derived from Eastern or Byzantine sources like mosaics and frescoes. In Latin Europe, images of the Virgin alone were abundant in the form of sculpture on church portals and in this way took on the symbol of the Mother Church itself. Exuding wisdom as she reigned over mankind, she was much larger than nearby figures outside the composition,

Figure 46. *Notre-Dame de la Belle Verriere.* Stained glass window from the south ambulatory, mid-12th century. Cathedral, Chartres, France. (Photo Credit: Réunion des Musées Nationaux/Art Resource, NY)

suggesting majesty. A crescent moon, the ancient symbol of chastity, sometimes appeared beneath her feet. She was typically veiled or, when enthroned, wore a crown. During the twelfth and thirteenth centuries, at the peak of cult devotion to her, she was referred to in mystical literature as *Regina Coeli*, Queen of Heaven. Artists very often depicted her in raptured majesty with crown, orb, and scepter, sometimes with and sometimes without the child (fig. 46). In the Latin West, one of the earliest depictions of this image is in the mosaics at Ravenna. The full-frontal view derived from the formality of Byzantine art, yet other versions show the Virgin either pointing to or embracing the child, symbolizing her role as Mother Church. The architectural features of her throne also typically connote the church and its personification by the Virgin.

The *Mater Dolorosa*, or Mother of Sorrows, shows the Virgin in grief, agonizing over the Passion of her son. She was typically shown with hands clasped and tears running down her face. Sometimes she was shown wearing the crown of thorns over her veil. Though often appearing alone as *Mater Dolorosa*, the term also applies to representations of her standing beside the cross or lamenting over the body of Christ lying in her lap, known as a Pietà, or Vesperbild in German (see fig. 7). These are among the most compelling of Christian images from the Middle Ages and would have provided an emotive experience for their intended audience. It was a particularly powerful focus for contemplation and private devotion. The Pietà served as a shocking counterpoint to the image of the Virgin and Child (see fig. 29). The German mystic Henry Suso (1295–1366) played a significant role through his writings in the cultivation and development of private devotion. Before an image of the *Pietà*, he imagines Mary to say:

> I took my tender Child on my lap and looked at Him, but He was dead; I looked at Him again and again, there was neither awareness nor voice. Behold my heart then died again, and could have shattered into a thousand pieces from those mortal wounds it received. It gave many inner bottomless sighs; the eyes had shed many heartbroken, bitter tears, my mien became utterly miserable.[1]

Suso responds to the Virgin's words with his own, addressing her directly:

> Alas, poor tender lady, I now beg you to offer me your tender Child, as it appeared when dead, placing it on the lap of my soul so that, according to my ability, I may be vouchsafed in a spiritual manner and in meditation that which befell you in a physical manner.

In the Germanic parts of Europe in particular, the *Mater Dolorosa* was a much-loved and much-used devotional theme.

Another theme, the Virgin of the Seven Sorrows, emerged during the late fifteenth century. Inaugurated by the Synod of Cologne in 1423 as a church festival, the Seven Sorrows were designated to form a counterpart to the already existing series of the Seven Joys.[2] In medieval art, these grievous events from the life of the Virgin may be depicted as vignettes surrounding the Virgin. This is especially common in books of hours. She is also sometimes depicted with seven swords piercing her breast or framing her head (fig. 47). This represents a literal reading of the prophecy of Simeon: "This child is destined to be a sign which men reject; and you too shall be pierced to the heart" (Luke 2:34–35).

Figure 47. *Seven Sorrows of the Virgin* (Office of Our Lady of Sorrows). The Virgin is shown with swords. Seven roundels depict the Presentation, Flight into Egypt, Christ in the Temple, Christ carrying the Cross, Crucifixion, Deposition, and Lamentation. At the foot, arms of the patron Nicolas Perrenot, Sieur de Granvelle. From the *Hours of the Sieur de Granvelle, France,* 1531–1532. Ink, tempera, and gold on vellum. The British Library, London. (Photo Credit: HIP/Art Resource, NY)

Figure 48. *Madonna della Misericordia* (Center Panel from a Polyptych painted for the Confratelli della Misericordia). Tempera and gilding on wood, ca. 1445–60. Piero della Francesca, Italian, Tuscany, ca. 1412–1492. Pinacoteca Comunale, Sansepolcro, Italy. (Photo Credit: Erich Lessing/Art Resource, NY)

The theme of the Seven Sorrows was especially prevalent in the art of northern Europe, where great emphasis was placed on the suffering of the Virgin. Her humanity as a woman and mother resonated deeply in the pietistic and mystical movements of Germany and the Low Countries. Identifying with her suffering became a principal focus of late medieval meditations. As a solitary figure without the swords but perhaps contemplating the Instruments of the Passion, she represents the Mother Church. Alone after the death of her son and after the disciples had fled, she is left to bear the sorrows of the world, an image in art called the Virgin of Pity.

A common image and class of paintings is that of the Virgin sheltering supplicants under her cloak. This composition is known as the Virgin of Mercy,
or *Madonna della Misericordia* (fig. 48). The Virgin's role in medieval piety was
that of intercessor before God for mankind at death or the Last Judgment.
However, she was also widely viewed as a mediator for the living, the subject
represented by this genre of images. Here, she appears alone without the infant. She is usually standing and wears an ample cloak which, with her arms
outstretched, becomes a protective cover or tent for the diminutive figures of
supplicants who kneel within. The cloak was a symbol of protection in antiquity, a meaning retained in the Latin West and Byzantine East. Very often the
supplicants represent every order of society—men and women, rich and poor,
clergy and secular. The theme of the Virgin of Mercy became widespread in

Figure 49. *Virgo Lactans*
(Virgin Nursing the Christ
Child). Tempera and gilding
on poplar. Francesco Ghissi,
Italian, The Marches, 14th
century. Pinacoteca, Vatican
Museums, Vatican State.
(Photo Credit: Scala/Art
Resource, NY)

the medieval West during the thirteenth century and declined in popularity during the sixteenth. It was a common image in monastic foundations and also in Christian charitable confraternities that identified with the Virgin of Mercy as their patron and protector, commissioning paintings as a votive and a reminder.

The image of the Virgin and Child is central to medieval art. It filled countless churches, private chapels, and roadside shrines throughout Christendom in the form of sculpture, painting, fresco, mosaic, and stained glass. Though representing a common theme in medieval art, there is a great deal of variety within the genre. The Virgin with her child may be shown standing or enthroned. There are multiple variations of pose, and the child typically held a variety of objects, such as fruit, flowers, or birds, to provide nuanced symbolic

Figure 50. *Virgo Lactans* (Virgin Nursing the Christ Child). Oil on panel (32.4 x 25.4 cm). Attributed to Hugo van der Goes, Netherlandish, ca. 1420–82. The Philadelphia Museum of Art. John G. Johnson Collection, 1917. (Photo Credit: The Philadelphia Museum of Art/Art Resource, NY)

meaning. Among the most ancient of these types is the *Virgo lactans,* the image of the Virgin suckling the infant Christ Child (fig. 49). It appears as early as the third century in fresco in the Roman catacombs. In the fourteenth century the *Virgo lactans* became a cult image in the many Italian churches that claimed to possess as holy relics some of the Virgin's milk. In this composition, the Virgin may either be seated or standing. Typically the child takes the breast in a naturalistic way. The breast may be discreetly hidden within the Virgin's draperies, or in some versions the breast may be wholly or partly visible. In Netherlandish painting of the fifteenth and early sixteenth centuries, scenes of the Virgin and Child are often set against a realistic background representing a detailed church interior or a domestic setting (fig. 50). The theme seems to have disappeared following the Council of Trent (1545–63), which objected to depictions of undue nudity with respect to sacred persons.

The Virgin and Child with a book was a common variation during the fifteenth century. In this version, the book is held either by the Virgin or the child. If held by the Virgin, the child may point to its open pages, suggestive of a foretelling of his Passion as written in the Gospels. An exquisite and emotive example is to be found in the Metropolitan Museum of Art, New York (fig. 51). This enthroned Virgin and Child is among the finest works of Claus de Werve. The Virgin's hair and the dramatic folds of her mantle provide a striking example of Burgundian sculpture as it emerged under Claus Sluter and Claus de Werve in the period of the first two dukes. The piece retains its original color. It was presented to the Convent of the Poor Clares at Poligny in Burgundy by Duke John the Fearless. The convent was established by the duke at his wife's urging. The sculpture was probably commissioned between June 1415 and October 1417, when the duke donated land and buildings to the convent. The book is traditionally the book of wisdom when held by the Virgin. It identifies the Virgin as *Mater Sapientiae,* or Mother of Wisdom. When held by the child, the book represents the Gospels.

Figure 51. *Seated Virgin and Child.* Polychromed limestone (H. 135 cm), ca. 1415–17. Claus de Werve, Netherlandish, active at the Burgundian Court, d. 1439. The Metropolitan Museum of Art, NY. Rogers Fund, Inv. 33.23. (Photo credit: Image copyright © The Metropolitan Museum of Art/ Art Resource, NY)

A type that became known through northern painting of the fourteenth century is called the Virgin of Humility. Its characteristic feature is that the Virgin is seated on the ground or perhaps on a cushion as an act of humility and not on a throne. Humility was regarded by medieval theologians as the root virtue from which the others grew. It was considered a much-cherished virtue of the Virgin, from whom Christ grew, and an exemplar to mankind. In a painting of this subject by Fra Angelico (fig. 52), the image of Mary recalls the

Figure 52. *Virgin of Humility.*
Tempera on panel (99 x 49
cm), ca. 1435–45. Fra Angelico,
act. Florence, ca. 1400–1455.
Fundación Colección Thyssen-
Bornemisza, Pedralbes

feminine ideal of beauty promoted by International Gothic art. The painting is noteworthy for its luminous palette in which brilliant shades of red, blue, and gold are harmoniously combined. The faces of Mary and her infant are rendered with deep sweetness and spirituality, and their gestures and poses are depicted with great naturalism typical of the interest of the age in realistic representation.

Toward the end of the Middle Ages, the Virgin and Child are sometimes depicted in a rose bower or before a trellis of roses that form an enclosed space (fig. 53). The enclosed garden thus formed, known as the *hortus conclusus,* became a symbol of Mary's virginity. The rose itself held symbolic meaning in Christian art: the red rose symbolized the blood of the martyrs, while the white symbolized purity. Christian tradition states that Jesus Christ

Figure 53. *Madonna of the Rosary.* Oil on panel. Martin Schongauer, German (active Comar), ca. 1448–91. Pinacoteca Nazionale, Bologna. (Photo Credit: Alinari/Art Resource, NY)

was conceived to Mary miraculously and without disrupting her virginity by the Holy Spirit, the third person of the Holy Trinity. As such, Mary in late medieval and Renaissance art, illustrating the long-held doctrine of her perpetual virginity, as well as the Immaculate Conception, was shown in or near a walled garden or yard. This was a representation of her "closed off" womb, which was to remain untouched, and also of her being protected, as by a wall, from sin. In the *Grimani Breviary*, for example, scrolling labels identify the objects emblematic of the Immaculate Conception: the enclosed garden (*hortus conclusus*), the tall cedar (*cedrus exalta*), the well of living waters (*puteus aquarum viventium*), the olive tree (*oliva speciosa*), the fountain in the garden (*fons hortorum*), and the rosebush (*plantatio rosae*). Not all actual medieval *horti conclusi* strove to include all these details; the olive tree in particular was unknown in northern European gardens.

A large number of objects were introduced into images of the Virgin and Child by artists, especially in the fifteenth and sixteenth centuries, as a means of conveying religious meaning. These objects were held either by the Virgin or the child or else placed on the ground nearby. Some of these may be considered attributes of the Virgin, such as the lily, which was especially used in scenes depicting the Annunciation. Since antiquity, the lily has been a symbol of purity, a quality reinforced by its white color. An olive branch, an emblem of peace, was occasionally substituted for the lily. The Tree of Jesse, taking the form of a meandering vine or branch, conveys the genealogy of Christ back to his ancestors King David and his father, Jesse. This branch, often with flowers, became an attribute of the Virgin, the human stock from which Christ grew (fig. 54).

More commonly, the Christ Child is represented with a symbolic object in hand, such as fruit or a bird. The apple, perhaps the most common of these, is the fruit of the Tree of Knowledge, an allusion to Christ as the redeemer of mankind from original sin. It signifies Christ as a second Adam. The inference is also understood by Mary, the new Eve, who grasps her son's fate from the moment of his birth. Grapes held by the child symbolize the Eucharistic wine and therefore the blood of Christ. Cherries held in the hand convey the "fruit of paradise," a reward for virtuousness and a symbol of heaven. The pomegranate was usually used by artists to signify the Resurrection. A bird held in the hand was symbolic of the human soul (fig. 55). In antiquity, the soul of man was symbolized by a bird, which flew away at his death. There are numerous such symbolic attributes in Western art used in connection with the image of the Virgin and Child of which these form a representative sample.

A common variant on the theme of the Virgin and Child was the addition of other figures, principally saints but occasionally donors. These exist in painting, sculpture, fresco, and other media. Typically the Virgin either stands or sits with her child in her arms while flanked on either side by two or more saints. The composition can take the form of an altarpiece in which the saints occupy separate compartments or that of a single panel on which all of the figures are represented together. In the latter instance, the figures form a unified representation known as the *Sacra Conversazione,* or holy conversation, in which the saints either stand or kneel around the often-seated Virgin and are in attendance of her (fig. 56). The identities of the saints in such paintings frequently serve as a clue to its provenance. The patron who commissioned the work could choose from among countless saints. Selections were often related to a specific church or confraternity with which he or she may have

Figure 54. *The Jesse Tree: Leaf from the Berthold Sacramentary.* Tempera on vellum. Germany, Abbey of Weingarten, ca. 1215. The Pierpont Morgan Library, NY. MS. M.710, f.112. (Photo Credit: The Pierpont Morgan Library/Art Resource, NY)

Figure 55. *Madonna and Child Enthroned*. Tempera on panel. Bernardo Daddi, Italian, ca. 1280–1348. Accademia, Florence. (Photo Credit: Finsiel/Alinari/Art Resource, NY)

been associated, to a specific religious order, or to the patron saint of a specific city or guild. Personal patron saints of the donor were often included in the composition as a testament to the patron's devotion. Thus, saints of different ages appear together regardless of the time in which they actually lived and died. Works bearing this theme and produced for a monastic order typically featured saints associated with that order. For example, the Franciscans feature Saints Francis, Clare, Anthony of Padua, and other saints emblematic of the order. Other reasons for choosing specific saints from the many thousands may be that those saints personified certain moral or intellectual attributes valued by the donor. Devotional images of the *Sacra Conversazione* may have also

Figure 56 *Sacra Conversazione* (from the *Altarpiece of Saint John the Baptist and Saint John the Evangelist*). Oil on oak panel (1,173.6 x 173.3 cm), 1474–79. Hans Memling, Netherlandish, 1425/40–1494. Memling Museum, Sint-Janshospitaal, Bruges. (Photo Credit: Erich Lessing/Art Resource, NY)

been commissioned and donated to a church or monastery out of gratitude for a favor from heaven or the deliverance from illness or mishap.

One of the most remarkable phenomena of the final century of the Middle Ages is the proliferation of books of hours, books made for the private devotion of the layperson. The popular appeal of books of hours during the fifteenth and early sixteenth centuries owed much to the fact that, at their heart, they were devoted to the veneration of the Virgin Mary. The core text and most important component of a book of hours was the Little Office of the Blessed Virgin Mary, generally appearing in the middle third of the book. Also called the Hours of the Virgin, this central text provided the rationale for their Latin name, *horae* ("hours"). Essentially the Hours of the Virgin constituted a sequence of prayers, hymns, and antiphons dedicated to Mary, the Mother of God. They were meant to be recited sequentially during the course of the day. Books of hours undoubtedly played a significant role in the late medieval cult of the Virgin, honoring Mary in the pivotal role of intercessor between man and God.

These manuscripts survive today in astonishing numbers, a fact suggesting that medieval men and women greatly treasured them. Aristocratic owners of books of hours frequently had their portraits painted in a position of pious repose reading and meditating with the volume's open pages before them. A panel from the *Altarpiece of the Last Judgment* (fig. 57), commissioned in 1434 by Nicolas Rolin, chancellor to Philip the Good, duke of Burgundy, and founder of the Hospital (Hotel-Dieu) of Beaune, shows his wife, Guigone de Salins, in prayer before her book of hours. Countless images in medieval art eloquently depict the use of such books in an aristocratic setting by their well-to-do owners. Such medieval paintings also capture the essence of the contemplative nature of private devotion, the essential purpose for which so many books of hours were made. They encapsulate a number of major considerations concerning medieval patronage, taste, and the intrinsic nature of piety and devotion during the fifteenth century. Books of hours were, throughout the fifteenth century, becoming increasingly fashionable among those members of the laity who could afford one. Eventually, middle-class members of the European burgher class could afford to buy more affordable, if less ostentatious, versions of them.

Books of hours, unlike psalters or breviaries, were made for the exclusive use of the layperson. They were used for private or family devotions within the home or private chapel (fig. 58). Their owners sometimes carried them to church where their texts could be recited prior to Mass as an aid to contemplation. As stated earlier, the texts of a book of hours consisted of a cycle of prayers, psalms, antiphons, hymns, and other devotional material arranged around the eight liturgical hours of the day. These devotions were modeled after the offices for the canonical hours practiced in monastic communities. This series of daily devotions, known as the Divine Office, would be said starting at Matins, around 2:30 A.M. and finally finishing with Compline in the evening.

Figure 57. *Guigone de Salins, Wife of Nicolas Rolin, Chancellor of the Dukes of Burgundy: Right panel from the reverse of the Altarpiece of the Last Judgment.* Tempera on panel, 1434. Roger van der Weyden, Netherlandish, ca. 1399–1464. Hotel-Dieu, Beaune. (Photo Credit: Erich Lessing/Art Resource, NY)

Figure 58. *Adoration of the Magi.* Fol. 78v. from *The Hours of Charles the Noble, King of Navarre.* Tempera and gold on vellum (19.4 x 13.7 cm). France, Paris, ca. 1405. The Cleveland Museum of Art. Mr. and Mrs. William H. Marlatt Fund 1964.40

Although the laity probably did not adhere completely to this rigorous schedule for their private devotions, their books were divided into the same eight parts. Some surviving books of hours are severely worn, suggesting their owners used them rigorously, while other books are in pristine condition, perhaps revealing that they were treasured more for their visual edification as works of art. Their direct inspiration was the breviary, a manuscript made exclusively for the use of the clergy and members of religious orders. While the owners of books of hours were thus meant to stop at eight set periods of the day to recite these devotions, unlike the clergy, they were not obligated to do so. It was strictly a voluntary act of piety. This then made up the central core of a book of hours to which were usually added other elements, such as a calendar, litanies, and suffrages. Books of hours were commonly decorated with a cycle of colorful miniatures and other illuminations to illustrate and embellish the book's textual components. Illustrations in books of hours included key images from the Virgin's life to support the texts of the Hours of the Virgin. An established iconography emerged early in the fifteenth century.

Since most of these images depicted Mary in conjunction with the childhood of Jesus, they are known as the Infancy Cycle (see fig. 58):

HOURS OF THE VIRGIN

HOUR	CORRESPONDING IMAGE
Matins	Annunciation
Lauds	Visitation
Prime	Nativity
Terce	Annunciation to the Shepherds
Sext	Adoration of the Magi
None	Presentation in the Temple
Vespers	Flight into Egypt, or Massacre of the Innocents
Compline	Coronation of the Virgin, Flight into Egypt, or Massacre of the Innocents

A common counterpart to the Infancy Cycle is the grouping of scenes of the Virgin with the adult Jesus. These include episodes related to Christ's Passion and death on the cross.[3]

In addition to the Hours of the Virgin, there appeared in most books of hours two special prayers to the Virgin. These were known after their *incipits* (opening words) as the *Obsecro te* ("I beseech you") and the *O intermerata* ("O immaculate Virgin"). These deeply moving prayers encapsulate the enduring devotion to the Virgin Mary as it relates to one's personal salvation. Typically, the iconography used in association with these prayers included a miniature of the Virgin and Child for the *Obsecro te* and an image of the Lamentation, or Pietà, for the *O intermerata*.

By the fifteenth century, books of hours had become the most prevalent book in the libraries of nobles or wealthy merchants. Those who could afford the expense commissioned the services of the finest artists to decorate their pages in luxurious fashion, and only the most extravagant and beautiful books of hours were commissioned for the highest aristocracy and royalty (fig. 59). With such fine workmanship involved in their production, they were also valued as precious works of art and family heirlooms. Private devotion increased in popularity during the fifteenth century largely as a result of increased lay literacy in Europe and the rise of a wealthy mercantile class able to afford such books. The quantity, design, and quality of the illuminations in a book of hours varied greatly according to the needs, whims, wealth, and taste of the person who commissioned it. However, it should be borne in mind that their core texts and illustrations were associated with the veneration of the Virgin Mary.

The final scene in the life of the Virgin, following her death and Assumption, is her coronation in heaven. The Coronation of the Virgin was a common

Figure 59. *The Crucifixion.*
Fol. 72v. from *The Hours of
Queen Isabella the Catholic
of Spain,* ca. 1497–1500.
Tempera and gold on vel-
lum (22.5 x 15.2 cm). Master
of the First Prayerbook of
Maximilian I and others.
Flanders, Ghent, and Bru-
ges, ca. 1500. The Cleveland
Museum of Art. Leonard C.
Hanna Jr. Fund 1963.256

subject on the sculpted portals of thirteenth-century French cathedrals. It was
also well known in most painted media, such as altarpieces and illuminations
in devotional and liturgical manuscripts (fig. 60), during the late Middle Ages
and Renaissance. In this role, the Virgin becomes the personification of the
church itself. The subject, not based on biblical texts, probably derived from
the Apocrypha, forming a well-established part of her iconography after the
thirteenth century. It essentially features the Virgin seated beside her son who
is placing the crown on her head. Both are typically seated on architectural
thrones with canopies. Alternatively, the Virgin kneels before Christ as he
places the crown on her head. A variation in Italian art is for God the Father
to crown the Virgin. In painting, the scene often takes place in the celestial
realm with the Virgin and Christ surrounded by the ranks of angels and saints
who witness the act. Such scenes are frequently painted in a rich palette of
colors to capture the great sanctity and ethereal quality of the occasion. Artists
traditionally show the Virgin richly robed in beautiful fabrics. The attendant
figures may also include the patriarchs and fathers of the church. Some of the

angels may play musical instruments, suggestive of the great joy, richness, and celebratory nature of this occasion.

One of the great movements in northern art of the fifteenth century was toward naturalism. While the Italians were generalists, interested in the universals underlying the physical world, the northerners, in this case the Flemish, were literalistic, interested in the particular. While the Italians concentrated on anatomical structure and how it is revealed by shading, the Flemish artists were unsurpassed in the rendering of surface textures. While the Italians used Brunelleschi's linear perspective, the Flemish approached perspective empirically, by observing how objects appeared in the spatial world. For

Figure 60. *Coronation of the Virgin from the Hours of Etienne Chevalier.* Jean Fouquet, French, Tours, ca.1415/20–1481. Musée Condé, Chantilly, Ms71, folio 13r. (Photo Credit: Réunion des Musées Nationaux/Art Resource, NY)

Figure 61. *The Annunciation: Central Panel from The Mérode Altarpiece,* Oil on wood (64.1 x 63.2 cm), ca. 1425. Robert Campin, Netherlandish, ca. 1373–1444. The Metropolitan Museum of Art. The Cloisters Collection, NY (56.7). (Photo Credit: Image copyright © The Metropolitan Museum of Art/Art Resource, NY)

northern artists, the Virgin was progressively viewed in terms of her humanity, as a noble woman or else as a member of the merchant class depicted in the realistic surrounds of a comfortable Flemish or Dutch home (see fig. 42). A masterful example of this impulse is the *Mérode Altarpiece* (fig. 61), a triptych painted between 1425 and 1428 by Robert Campin and commissioned for private use. Campin was not a court painter but made his livelihood painting for his well-to-do fellow townsmen. In the central panel of the *Mérode Altarpiece,* which depicts the Annunciation, one of the most sacred and spiritual subjects in Marian iconography, the viewer experiences the spatial depth created by the "picture window effect," as if peering into the interior of the room from outside. Within the room are all the domestic comforts that would have been valued by the Flemish burgher culture: a hearth with an elaborate fire screen and andirons, both representing warmth and comfort. Leaded glass windows, a significant expense, appear in the background. Elsewhere, a brass lavabo (for washing) hangs within a niche with a towel nearby. On the table is a beautiful Florentine ewer with an oak leaf pattern. The urban merchant class would have treasured such a valuable piece of earthenware from Italy.

Within this realistic setting, Mary reposes gracefully against a cushioned ornate bench as she reads devoutly from her book of hours. On the table to her right, another book lies open. Mary seems unaware of the angel Gabriel who approaches from her right. In this domestic interior, Mary becomes representative of the urban middle-class woman, precisely the clientele for which this painting was intended. The challenge for the artist was to transfer a supernatural event—the Annunciation—into the everyday domestic world of early fifteenth-century Flanders. To accomplish this, Campin used the technique of disguised symbolism so that everything shown in the painting, however humble or commonplace, bears some hidden meaning. The eye is drawn in succession to every object within the room, each rendered with extreme clarity and realism. Everything in the room is of equal importance, and symbolic meaning may be found in most of these objects. The lily on the table, for example, has three flowers. Two flowers are open and one is about to bloom. These represent the Father, Son, and Holy Spirit/Ghost, with Jesus, whose birth is the subject of the painting, about to "flower." The plume of smoke rising from the candle suggests a holy presence, and the lily symbolizes the Virgin's chastity. The book and the scroll on the table represent the Old and New Testaments and the role of Mary and the Christ Child in fulfilling biblical prophecy. The lion finials on the bench ends may reference the Seat of Wisdom or the Throne of Solomon. The washing accoutrements in the rear of the room, the lavabo and towel, may allude to the arrangements of the piscine used by officiating priests to wash their hands during Mass. Indeed the table in the center of the room may represent an altar with the Archangel Gabriel wearing the vestments of a deacon. The goal appears to be one of making sacred symbols look like part of the natural world. The union of symbolism and realism is characteristic of many fifteenth-century northern European paintings. It is a union that makes the secular world sacred and may help explain why donors wanted their portraits included in the altarpieces (and other religious paintings) they commissioned.

CHAPTER FIVE

Images of the Cross and the Crucifixion

he cross is one of the oldest and most universal of all symbols. It is the central image in Christian art, the unique symbol of Christ himself. In a broader sense, the cross has come to symbolize the Christian religion, and in the eyes of Christians, it is the emblem of atonement and the symbol of salvation and redemption through the Christian faith.

The Crucifixion (fig. 62), viewed as a narrative scene in Western art, has provided artists with a powerful subject used to decorate the walls of chapels, altar screens, pages of illuminated manuscripts, and stained glass windows of Gothic cathedrals, among other contexts. Even secular objects, such as domestic furniture, jewelry, and medieval arms and armor, have been engraved, embossed, cast, and carved with this emotive devotional image. Its place in the visual arts of western Europe—and especially in the Christian iconography of the Middle Ages—is fundamentally important. It is also necessary to distinguish between the Crucifixion scene (a narrative image) and the cross itself (a symbol). It should be noted that the cross occurs in art much earlier than Crucifixion scenes (fig. 63).

The death of Christ on the cross is the visual focus of Christian contemplation. The character of this image would vary from one age to another reflecting the prevailing climate of Christian thought and feeling. Pictorially, Christ's Crucifixion was not only understood by medieval and Renaissance

Figure 62. *The Crucifixion.* Oil and gold on panel (37.1 x 27.3 cm). Netherlands, ca. 1470. The Cleveland Museum of Art. Delia E. and L. E. Holden Funds 1931.449

artists as a historical event but also as an instructive and devotional instrument that could be portrayed in terms of its mystical, symbolic, and allegorical values. In this way, ecclesiastical art could express both doctrine and morality to its intended audience. Indeed, some artists, such as the painter Fra Angelico or the metalworker Roger of Helmarshausen, viewed their crafts as personal expressions of piety. The image of the crucified Christ could serve as a simple aid to devotion by portraying nothing but the solitary figure on the cross, as exemplified by a twelfth-century German bronze altar cross from Hildesheim (fig. 64). Or again, the image might attempt to narrate the Gospel story in a painting crowded with people, such as the complex composition by the German master of the Schlägel altarpiece (fig. 65).

Figure 63 (facing page). View of the central vault with the starry firmament and the symbols of the Evangelists. Mosaic, 425–26. Mausoleum of Galla Placidia, Ravenna. (Photo Credit: Scala/Art Resource, NY)

Figure 64 (left). *Altar Cross*. Gilt-bronze (H. 43.3 cm). Germany, Lower Saxony, Hildesheim, ca. 1175–90. The Cleveland Museum of Art. Purchase from the J. H. Wade Fund 1944.320

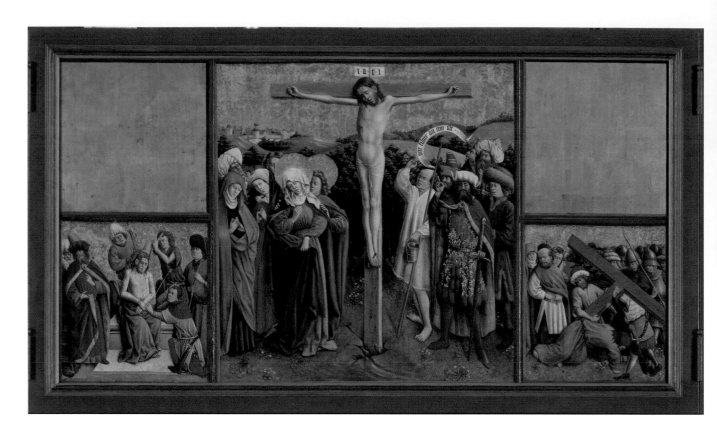

Figure 65. *The Crucifixion* (central panel from an altarpiece of the *Passion of Christ*). Oil and gold on wood panel (74.3 x 69.8 cm). Master of the Schlägel Altar, German, ca. 1440s. The Cleveland Museum of Art. Mr. and Mrs. William H. Marlatt Fund 1951.453

The early church avoided this subject, however. No image of the Crucifixion has survived from the monumental art of early Christian Rome, and none is known to us from written accounts. In Late Antiquity, realistic representations of Christ are generally confined to two versions. The first is that of a youthful, beardless Christ, draped and seated in a chair and perhaps holding a partially open scroll. This is Christ as philosopher. Such representations usually portray Christ seated among apostles, saints, martyrs, or deceased Christians, for, according to early Christian doctrine, Christ was the teacher of the "true philosophy," a belief carried over from Roman interest in pagan philosophy (see fig. 17). This version alludes to the Roman tradition of seated deity representations. The philosopher-deity type was later to develop into the seated Christ in Majesty used throughout medieval art (see figs. 43 and 44). A second version is that of Christ as the Good Shepherd (see fig. 15). Here, Christ is again shown as youthful and beardless—an Apollo-like figure—with large locks of hair in the Hellenistic fashion. He is dressed in a belted, sleeveless tunic and supports a ram on his shoulders. The youthful ram-bearing shepherd has a long tradition of pagan usage, but in Late Antiquity this image acquired a general philanthropic savior symbolism. As such, it was adopted by the Christians as the Good Shepherd—Christ as savior of the Christian flock as described in the Gospels of both John and Luke.

Nevertheless, the paucity of these three-dimensional sculptures, due in part to the Judeo-Christian fear of idolatry, rendered the acceptance of realistic art in the Byzantine Empire uneasy. As a viable alternative, a rich vocabulary of symbolic forms was to emerge. Thus, at a time when Christianity was a proscribed religion under the Romans, the Crucifixion of Christ was represented symbolically by the Lamb of God, or *Agnus Dei*, juxtaposed with a cross. The lamb is a biblical symbol of Christ, the roots of which extend back to Old Testament typology of sacrifice—for instance, Abel or Abraham. The durability of this early symbol of Christ's Crucifixion may be seen on the lid of an enamel casket produced in northern Germany in the twelfth century (fig. 66).

Even after the age of Constantine when Christians were permitted to practice their religion without interference, the cross was still represented without the figure of Christ. The image of the Crucifixion, that is to say the Calvary scene as we know it, is first found in the sixth century and represented on a few lead pilgrims' ampullae surviving from that period (fig. 67). Ampullae and other small flasks of this type were made during the earliest centuries of Christianity, probably in Jerusalem, for pilgrims who wanted to carry home with them a memento of their journey to the sacred sites of the Holy Land. These tiny vessels were usually filled with samples of the sacred oil that burned in the lamps of the shrines. These sacred shrines, which were housed within churches built by Emperor Constantine and his sons, were mostly destroyed when the Holy Land fell to the Muslims after 614. Once filled with the holy oil, the ampulla was worn around the pilgrim's neck as an amulet. It functioned not only as a personal souvenir from a pilgrimage but also as a way to ward off evil.

Figure 66. *Lid of a Casket with the Agnus Dei.* Gilt-copper and champlevé enamel on a core of wood (9.3 x 23.4 x 13.5 cm). Northern Germany or Denmark, early 12th century. The Cleveland Museum of Art. Purchase from the J. H. Wade Fund 1949.16

Figure 67. *Pilgrim's Ampulla with Crucifixion Scene.* Tin-lead alloy with leather fragments (H. 6.3 cm). Palestine, ca. 600. The Cleveland Museum of Art. John L. Severance Fund 1999.46

Though now difficult to see, the images found on the sides of lead pilgrims' ampullae invariably consist of scenes relating to the life of Christ, and by extension to the holy sites, or *loca sancta,* where the events took place. Cast into the ampulla's sides are scenes of Christ's Crucifixion (fig. 67) and Ascension. The use of such sacred images on these vessels illustrates early Christians' perception that images carried divine power. In this way, pilgrims' ampullae, along with their contents, helped transport abroad the sanctity of the Holy Land in a tangible and visible manner. These humble objects depict some of the earliest images of the Crucifixion known to Western art. The ampulla was cast as two separate halves and was then soldered together. On one side, the ampulla portrays Golgotha, or Calvary, where the Crucifixion took place. Its inscription reads, "Oil of the Wood of Life from the Holy Sites." This undoubtedly refers to a relic of the True Cross, known to have been kept in the Martyrium, near the Church of the Holy Sepulchre in Jerusalem. The wood of the cross was literally touched against the flasks containing the lamp oil in order to sanctify it.[1]

For many centuries, the West, under Byzantine influence, represented Christ alive with open eyes on the cross, a triumphant Savior wearing a royal crown. A twelfth-century French corpus of Christ, now in the Cleveland Museum of Art, is a late expression of this type (fig. 68). Now lacking its arms and crown, and no longer attached to its cross, this figure still reveals a monumental quality and quiet dignity. A few centuries later, artists and theologians had developed a

new iconography of Christ crucified on the cross. This newer version presented the emaciated figure of the Redeemer with his head fallen on one shoulder and wearing not a royal crown but a crown of thorns. It showed a dying, suffering man who evoked feelings of compassion and loyalty among viewers. Such figures of the distressed Christ seek the worshippers' sympathetic identification. This newer version, illustrated by a middle-Rhenish example (fig. 69), probably carved in Cologne about 1380, was intended to convey in vivid terms the physical suffering of Christ at the moment of his death.

This Colognese figure, seen in contradistinction to the earlier French corpus, illustrated a radical shift of conception—from the Byzantine triumphant savior to a more human Christ. Artists began to see the Redeemer, in all his frailty and suffering, in a more literal interpretation of the narrative in the Gospels of Christ's Passion. The fourteenth-century German mystic Heinrich Suso wrote extensively on Christ's sufferings in passionate and emotive terms. In his widely read *Little Book of Eternal Wisdom*, Suso recalls a mystical vision he had in which the Savior describes his sufferings:

When I was suspended on the high branch of the Cross with boundless love, for the sake of thee and all men, My whole form was wretchedly

Figure 68 (left). *Crucified Christ*. Polychromed wood (H. 111.1 cm). France, 12th century. The Cleveland Museum of Art. Leonard C. Hanna Jr. Bequest 1980.1

Figure 69 (right). *Crucified Christ (Crucifixus Dolorosus)*. Walnut (H. 47.5 cm). Germany, Cologne, ca. 1380. The Cleveland Museum of Art. Andrew R. and Martha Holden Jennings Fund 1981.52

disfigured, My clear eyes were dimmed and lost their lustre; My divine ears were filled with mockery and insult, My noble sense of smell was assailed by an evil stench, My sweet mouth with a bitter draught, My gentle sense of touch with hard blows. Then I could not find a place of rest in the whole world, for My Divine head was bowed down by pain and torment; My joyful throat was rudely bruised; My pure countenance was defiled with spittle; the clear color of My cheeks turned wan and pallid. Look, My fair form was . . . as though I were a leper. . . . All my tender limbs were immovably riveted to the narrow halter. . . . My dying body was covered with blood, which was a distressful sight. Behold, a lamentable thing: My young, fair healthy body began to grow grey, to dry up and wither.[2]

By meditating on the physical suffering of Christ, Suso believed that the faithful could share in his pain. Such personalized devotions called for an art that spoke directly of the Redeemer's suffering.

Beginning in the twelfth century, artists began to include other figures from the Gospels, figures who would become regular features of the Crucifixion image, both in the monumental and decorative arts: the Virgin Mary, Saint John the Evangelist, the centurion, the sponge bearer, the two thieves, and the soldiers casting lots. Most iconographical features of the Crucifixion relate closely to aspects of Christian doctrine. Christians believe that by sacrificing himself on the cross, Christ brought about the possibility of man's redemption, that is to say his delivery from the original sin of Adam, which all mankind inherited. Medieval writers therefore set out to establish "historical" links between the Fall and the Crucifixion, maintaining, for example, that the cross was made from the very wood of the Tree of Knowledge in the Garden of Eden (or from one that grew from its seed) and that Adam's burial place was at the site of the Crucifixion. The skull commonly represented at the foot of the cross in Crucifixion scenes, therefore, alludes not merely to Golgotha, "the place of the skull," but represents Adam's own skull (see fig. 62). Adam's relevance to the Crucifixion through the doctrine of the Redemption, and hence the juxtaposition of his skull at the foot of the cross, is first seen in the ninth century and recurs thereafter throughout Christian art in most media. The skull is frequently sprinkled with the blood that drips from Christ's body. This symbolic washing away of Adam's sin would become a particular feature of Counter-Reformation painting at the end of the sixteenth century, at which time the skull was sometimes depicted upside down as a chalice, actually catching the blood.

Christ's blood, which was shed on the cross, was understood early in the Middle Ages to have redemptive powers, a concept embodied in the sacrament of Communion. Hence it became customary to represent the stream of blood that issued from the wound in Christ's side as being caught in a chalice, the Eucharistic vessel, sometimes by attending angels (fig. 70). In these and other ways, the image of the Crucifixion assumed a didactic role, serving as a reminder of Christian teaching.

The subject as a whole lends itself to symmetrical treatment, and there is a marked tendency toward the use of figures in pairs, one balanced against the other on either side of the cross, for example the Virgin and Saint John. We should note also the moral distinction between the right and left sides: good on the right side of Christ and evil on his left, as for instance the positioning of the penitent and impenitent thieves.

Figure 70. *The Crucifixion: Leaf from a Missal.* Tempera and gold on vellum (22.9 x 15.9 cm). Bohemia or Silesia, ca. 1480. The Cleveland Museum of Art. Mr. and Mrs. William H. Marlatt Fund 1949.205

In Roman times, crucifixion was widely used as a form of capital punishment, reserved for baser criminals and slaves. It was probably carried out in a manner different from that generally depicted in Western art. The footrest, or *suppedaneum,* for instance, was an invention of medieval artists. Also, though it is customary for the two thieves to be shown tied to the cross, in reality they probably would have been nailed. In art up to the thirteenth century, the usual number of nails depicted was four (including one for each foot); thereafter, with few exceptions, it was three (one foot nailed over the other). The only reference to Christ's nails in the Gospels is by Doubting Thomas in the Gospel of Saint John. In antiquity, an inscription, or *titulus,* stating the nature of the condemned man's offense was hung around his neck as he was led to execution and was afterward affixed to the head of the cross. The Evangelist John (19:19–20) describes how Pilate wrote an inscription in Hebrew, Latin, and Greek to be fastened to Christ's cross; it read, "Jesus of Nazareth, King of the Jews." In Renaissance art, it is usually given in Latin only: IESUS NAZARENUS REX IUDAEORUM, abbreviated to INRI.

As already indicated, artists of the later Middle Ages and Renaissance depicted Christ dead on the cross, a departure from the earlier Byzantine convention. The Gospel of Saint John states that Christ bowed his head at the moment of death. His head thus inclines on his shoulder (see figs. 62, 64, 65, and 70), nearly always to the right, indicating the moral symmetry of the image (the right being an indication of good). The Crown of Thorns became widely depicted from the mid-thirteenth century after King Louis IX of France acquired the holy relic from Baldwin II, the Latin Emperor of Constantinople. It was subsequently enshrined in the Sainte-Chapelle in Paris. Until the Counter-Reformation, the Crown of Thorns is seldom omitted in art.

The medieval church debated whether Christ would have been crucified naked on the cross, though those condemned in Roman times generally were. In the earliest depictions of the crucified Christ, he wears a long sleeveless garment in the East (see fig. 67). Elsewhere he is shown wearing a thin band of cloth, the *subligaculum.* Either could be correct historically. There is, however, no precedent for the familiar loincloth, or *perizonium* (see figs. 62, 64–65), an invention of artists in the early Middle Ages.

All four Gospels relate that two thieves were crucified with Christ, one on each side. Luke, however, adds that one thief rebuked the other and repented. As a consequence, Christ promised him salvation. Art, following Luke, distinguished between the penitent and impenitent thief. The good thief, on Christ's right (the "good" side), sometimes appears as composed and peaceful, whereas the other thief appears anguished. The soul of the good was sometimes shown being borne away by angels; that of the bad by demons. In Byzantine painting, the thief to the right is often portrayed as a gray-haired man with a round beard; the thief to the left as young and beardless. However, these portrayals were not always followed in the European West. While the early Italian Renaissance tended to follow the Byzantine practice of depicting the thieves, like Christ, nailed to their crosses, these artists conformed to the medieval custom of relating size to sanctity, depicting their crosses smaller than Christ's. In order to differentiate clearly between Christ and the thieves, Western artists commonly showed the thieves bound, not nailed, to their crosses (fig. 71). Moreover, their crosses, unlike Christ's, became T-shaped, or *crux commissa.*

Around the foot of the cross, Western artists began to represent the various persons described by the Gospels as being present at the Crucifixion. The Evangelist John states that one of the soldiers pierced Christ's side after he was already dead. Much legend and speculation surrounded this soldier. He was named Longinus (from the Greek word for lance) and came to be identified with the centurion in the synoptic Gospels (not mentioned by John), who exclaimed, "Truly this man was the son of God." In a painted panel from the Schlägel Altar dating to about 1440, Longinus appears to the immediate right of the cross, clothed in white, with those words in Latin emanating from his mouth in a banderole (see fig. 65). He supports a lance in his left arm. The *Golden Legend* tells us that Longinus was later baptized, martyred, and canonized. Artists often keep these identities separate, showing both a soldier piercing the side of Christ, and a centurion in armor, perhaps on horseback. All four Gospels mentioned that a sponge soaked in vinegar and fixed to the end of a pole was offered to Christ just before he died. Legend states the sponge bearer's name was Stephaton, and he was regularly paired with Longinus in medieval art. The sponge bearer becomes somewhat rare in Renaissance art, but the sponge is often seen upraised on a pole among the soldiers' weapons.

Another theme that occurs throughout medieval and Renaissance art is that of the soldiers casting lots. John's account is the fullest and generally the most cited. Having crucified Christ, the soldiers divided his clothes into four parts— one for each soldier. Of the seamless tunic, woven in one piece, they decided not to tear it but to cast lots for it. In painting, they are either portrayed at the foot of the cross or at the corner of the picture. One soldier is in the act of throwing the dice while the others look on. Alternatively, they are sometimes shown quarreling, one about to cut the garment with a knife, while another tries to mediate. The number of soldiers varies and may be as few as three.

The most common composition throughout the Middle Ages is that of the Virgin and Saint John standing by the cross. This image was originally intended to express in visual terms the passage from Saint John's Gospel in which Christ, while he still lived, entrusted the Virgin to the care of the apostle John. The pattern became established in the West through the art of the Carolingian Renaissance. The Virgin stands on the right of Christ and Saint John on the left (see figs. 62, 70). Their heads may be inclined. The Virgin sometimes raises her left hand to her cheek, supporting the elbow with the

Figure 71. *The Crucifixion: Leaf from a Missal.* Tempera and gold on vellum (33.6 x 25.5 cm). Master of Otto van Moerdrecht, North Netherlands, ca. 1438–39. The Cleveland Museum of Art. Mr. and Mrs. William H. Marlatt Fund 1959.254

right hand, a traditional gesture of grief that dates back to Hellenistic times. Saint John may be depicted gazing upward at the face of Christ, who is generally represented as still living, in conformity with the Gospel account and with prevailing artistic convention. Later, as the living, triumphant figure on the cross gives way to the dead Christ with the wound in his side, the two figures below manifest grief in a more naturalistic manner, and the strict sense of the Gospel is lost. In the fourteenth century, the theme tended to be overtaken by that of the Virgin swooning (see fig. 71).

There is no biblical sanction for this incident, highly favored by Renaissance artists. The virgin swooning appears to be a creation of later medieval monastic preachers and mystical writers. In dwelling on the sorrows of the Virgin, they tended to assume that she was overcome with extreme anguish by the events of the Passion. It was said that she swooned three times: on the road to Calvary, at the Crucifixion, and after the descent from the cross. The change to the upright, stoically grieving figure of medieval art came about gradually. In earlier examples, the Virgin is still on her feet but supported by the holy women or by Saint John (see fig. 65). Eventually, however, she was sometimes shown completely collapsed on the ground (see fig. 71). The motif was explicitly condemned by the Council of Trent, which directed artists to John's words: "Near the cross *stood* his mother" (John 19:25; emphasis mine). Consequently, she is rarely seen kneeling or on the ground after the second half of the sixteenth century.

The Evangelists mention the holy women, the companions of the Virgin, but the varying descriptions are difficult to reconcile. Mary whom John calls the wife of Clopas was said to be the same as Mary whom Matthew and Mark call the mother of James and Joseph. Similarly, Salome, mentioned by Mark, was regarded as the same person as the mother of Zebedee's children in Matthew. These two, together with Mary Magdalene, are commonly known as the Three Marys. Artists of the Middle Ages and Renaissance portrayed them in varying ways. In art, their numbers vary, but they are generally three or four. Their appearance is not clearly differentiated except for Mary Magdalene, who, in early Renaissance art, wears red. It was not until the Renaissance that Mary of Magdalene came to be distinguished from the other holy women. In early works she may sometimes be recognized by her red cloak among those supporting the swooning Virgin, but her typical role throughout Renaissance and Counter-Reformation art shows her as a separate figure, often richly attired and with her usual copious hair.

From about the mid-fifteenth century, another version of the Crucifixion may be found in which saints, regardless of the age in which they lived, are assembled together before the cross in much the same manner as the *Sacra Conversazione*, which came into being at about this time (fig. 72). This devotional treatment of the subject is found principally in Italian art. The saints, who can

be recognized by their customary attributes, may be the patrons of the city or church, or founders of the religious order, for which the work was commissioned. Saints often depicted at the Crucifixion include Francis of Assisi, Dominic, Augustine, Benedict, and Bernard of Clairvaux. Jerome and Catherine of Alexandria, perhaps as patrons of learning, are also included. Kneeling in the foreground are Saints Jerome and Dominic. Saints Sebastian and Roch are also often invoked as protectors against the plague, often accompanying a kneeling donor, signifying that the work was a votive offering to the church in thanksgiving for the donor's escape from sickness. John the Baptist may be present either as one of the tutelary saints or for his place in the scheme of Christian belief as the prophet of Christ's divinity and redemptive sacrifice. The Virgin and Saint John the Evangelist are nearly always standing behind and at the sides of the crucified Christ.

Patrons who commissioned works of art, whether sculptural or pictorial, generally had no compunction about having their own image represented in religious subjects during the Middle Ages and Renaissance. Patrons often had their images painted or sculpted, for instance, kneeling before a seated Madonna and Child—a symbolic act of devotion and piety. Crucifixion scenes served this purpose equally well and proved very popular with both clergy and laypersons alike. Consequently, such images indicate who commissioned the image and also proclaim, to all who see it, this person's devotion to Christ. From about the fourteenth century onward, kneeling kings, dukes, duchesses, priests, nuns, bishops (fig. 73; see also fig. 70), cardinals, and popes proliferate as patrons of devotional images.

A theme to which special significance was attached in later medieval art was the wound in Christ's side. Much of the symbolism surrounding this was due to Saint Augustine. The blood and water, which, according to John, issued from the wound, was conceived by Augustine to represent the sacraments of Eucharist and baptism. Just as Eve was fashioned from a rib taken from Adam's side, so the two main Christian sacraments flowed from the side of Christ, the "New Adam." Thus, in symbolic language, the church was born from the wound. In the later Middle Ages, the figure of Adam, perhaps emerging from the tomb, is occasionally seen below the cross, holding a chalice in which he catches the redeeming blood. From the fourteenth through the sixteenth centuries, one or more angels, each bearing a chalice, are similarly engaged floating beside the cross, one at each wound (see fig. 70). The wound is generally on the right side of the body, the so-called good side and, according to Augustine, the side of "eternal life." By the early seventeenth century, this symbolism was forgotten and the wound appears on either side.

Another regular feature in medieval crucifixion images is that of the sun and the moon, one found on either side of the cross. They can be plainly seen on an eleventh-century German ivory plaque (fig. 74). These symbols survived

Figure 72 (facing page). *Crucifixion with Saints.* Oil on panel. Pietro Perugino, Italian, 1448–1523. S. Agostino, Siena. (Photo Credit: Scala/Art Resource, NY)

Figure 73. *Crucifixion with Kneeling Donor.* Oil on wood transferred on canvas (34 x 26 cm). Konrad Witz, German (active Basel), 1400/10–1445/46. Gemäldegalerie, Staatliche Museen zu Berlin, Berlin, Inv. 1656. (Photo Credit: Bildarchiv Preussischer Kulturbesitz/ Art Resource, NY)

into the early Renaissance but are seldom seen after the fifteenth century. Their origin, however, is ancient. In antiquity, it was customary to represent the sun and moon in images of the pagan sun gods of Persia and Greece, a practice that was carried into Roman times on coins depicting the emperors. The practice found its way into primitive Christian art through the festival of Christmas, which evolved from an existing pagan feast celebrating the birth of the sun. When artists began to depict Christ on the cross, the symbols of the moon and sun were already established in the Bible and accepted by theologians. According to the synoptic Gospels, a darkness fell over the whole land at midday and lasted until three in the afternoon. The eclipse might simply be a sign that the heavens went into mourning at the death of the Savior; but

Figure 74. *Plaque from a Portable Altar with the Crucifixion.* Walrus ivory (5.1 x 9.5 cm). Germany, Rhine Valley, mid-11th century. The Cleveland Museum of Art. Gift of Arnold Seligmann, Rey and Company 1922.359

more specifically, according to Augustine, the sun and the moon symbolized the prefigurative relationship of the two Testaments: the Old (the moon) was only to be understood by the light shed upon it by the New (the sun). The sun appears on Christ's right; the moon on his left.

The two allegorical figures, sometimes seen on either side of the cross and symbolizing the Ecclesia and the Synagogue, belong strictly to the Middle Ages and are included here as another indication of how medieval artists observed the "moral symmetry" of the crucifixion image. Matthew (27:51) tells how, at the moment of Christ's death, "the curtain of the Temple was torn in two from top to bottom." This, in the eyes of Christian commentators of the Middle Ages, marked the end of the Old Law and the beginning of the New—the triumph of the Ecclesia over the Synagogue. On the lid of a twelfth-century enamel casket in the Cleveland Museum of Art, these allegorical figures appear immediately flanking the cross (fig. 75). On the outside are the Virgin and Saint John. The Ecclesia, on the right of the cross, is crowned and holds a chalice in which she catches the Redeemer's blood. The Synagogue, on the left of the cross (the viewer's right), is blindfolded, and her crown falls from her inclined head. The tables of the law may likewise fall from her hands. These figures first became widespread during the Carolingian period and are found later in the sculpture and stained glass of the cathedrals of twelfth- and thirteenth-century Europe.

The eminent French art historian Émile Mâle said, "Art in the Middle Ages is a script." Thus, every complicated assembly of images—whether a cathedral portal, a painted triptych, or a carved ivory plaque—represents a certain amount of book work on the part of the artist or patron. The sculpture of a cathedral portal, for example, was almost certainly created according to a program laid

Figure 75. *Lid from a Reliquary Casket with the Crucified Christ flanked by Ecclesia and Synagogue.* Champlevé enamel and gilt-copper (21.3 x 9.2 cm). Germany, Lower Saxony, Hildesheim, ca. 1180. The Cleveland Museum of Art. Purchase from the J. H. Wade Fund and the Fanny Tewksbury King Collection by Exchange 1949.431

down by a scholar, probably a canon, who was likely inspired by a text. To this extent, crucifixion images will express some aspect of contemporary thought as well as religious feeling as gleaned from scripture and patristic literature.

Through the centuries, many and varied forms of the cross have evolved (the Latin cross, the Greek cross, the patriarchal cross, the tau cross, Saint Andrew's cross, and so forth). Some scholars have estimated that there are over four hundred forms of the cross, fifty or sixty of which are in common use today. Yet the cross referred to in the New Testament, the cross of Christ's Crucifixion, was not the original model for the cross we know today. The form of the cross first used as a symbol for Christianity in the early centuries after the death of Christ was derived from the first letter of Christ's name in Greek, the *chi*, an X-shaped letter (fig. 76). Early Christians used this instantly recognizable symbol to mark everything—food, cups, plates, oil lamps, furniture, clothing, and especially sarcophagi—as a symbol of devotion to their faith (see fig. 13). Variations on the *chi*, particularly geometric variations, were quick to arise. It was, however, the combination of the *chi* with the *rho* (the second letter of Christ's name in Greek) and the elaboration on this combination that produced the first of what gave rise to hundreds of permutations.

The symbolic and emblematic aspects of the cross are thus considerable. For instance, the cross, sometimes represented with a chalice, is the attribute of Faith personified; when it is shown resting on a book, it becomes a symbol of the Bible. The devotion to the infant Christ during the later Middle Ages was expressed in a number of themes showing the Christ Child in relation to the cross, as if anticipating his death. The cross in the form of a crucifix assumed a votive function as a simple object of personal or private devotion, both in secular and ecclesiastical contexts. The crucifix was simply the three-dimensional image of Christ on the cross. These objects gained popularity with laypersons as personal devotional objects for the home or private chapel. In art, the crucifix often becomes an attribute of certain saints, such as Charles Borromeo, Francis of Assisi, Mary Magdalene, and a number of others.

Figure 76. *Monogram of Christ (Chi-Rho or Chrismon)*. Gold with garnets (14.8 x 12.1 cm). Byzantium, Syria, 6th or 7th century. The Cleveland Museum of Art. Gift of Lillian M. Kern 1965.551

These hidden meanings have been all but lost to modern visitors to sacred buildings and museums. Medieval men and women, however, were familiar with the shades of meaning represented by their religious art and architecture. William Langland, author of the fifteenth-century English epic poem *Piers Plowman,* observed of church art that "these paintings and images are poor men's books."[3] This schooling may have been informally offered through the pulpit by a parish priest, or conversely through formal training in the monasteries, convents, cathedral schools, and—after 1200—the universities. Indeed, medieval Christian art is, as Mâle expressed, a "sacred script." It awaits deciphering by those who know its codes.

Notes

1. The Context and the Medieval Mind

1. Johann Huizinga, *The Waning of the Middle Ages* (New York: Anchor Books, 1989), 9–10. This work was published as a new edition in 1997 as *The Autumn of the Middle Ages*.

2. Musée Condé, Chantilly (Ms. 65/1284, fol. 2v.). See the facsimile edition, *Les Très Riches Heures du Duc de Berry, Musée Condé, Chantilly,* trans. Victoria Benedict (London: Thames and Hudson, 1969).

3. Huizinga, 9.

4. Musée Condé, Chantilly (Ms. 65/1284, fol. 10v.).

5. Cited in James Harpur, *Revelations, the Medieval World* (New York: Henry Holt and Company, 1995), 66.

6. *Très Riches Heures* (Musée Condé, Chantilly, Ms. 65/1284, fol. 129v.). The manuscript was left uncompleted at the death of Duke Jean de Berry. Its remaining folios were painted by Jean Colombe of Bourges in the late 1480s after the manuscript had fallen into the possession of the Duke of Savoy.

7. See William D. Wixom, *Medieval Sculpture at The Cloisters* (New York: The Metropolitan Museum of Art, 1988), 5–6.

8. See Henk van Os, *The Art of Devotion in the Late Middle Ages in Europe, 1300–1500* (Princeton, N.J.: Princeton Univ. Press, 1994), 158–72.

9. Letter from Bernard of Clairvaux to William of Cluny, in *The Complete Works of St. Bernard,* ed. Dom Jean Mabillon (1667; repr. Paris, 1690), n.p. This phrase also appears in his *De modo bene vivendi,* chap. 9.

2. The Early Christian and Byzantine Perception of Images

1. For a fuller discussion of the theological issues surrounding the iconoclastic debate, see Jaroslav Pelikan, *Imago Dei: The Byzantine Apologia for Icons* (Princeton, N.J.: Princeton Univ. Press, 1990).

2. Joseph D. Frendo, trans., *Agathias: The Histories in Corpus Fontium Historiae Byzantinae,* vol. 2A, Series Berolinensis, Berlin; New York: de Gruyter, 1975.

3. Images of the Saints, Angels, and Holy Persons

1. A smaller version of the *Christ and Saint John* (34.5 cm) is now in the Liebieghaus-Museum alter Plastik in Frankfurt (Inv. 1447). It originated from the former Dominican convent at Adelhausen in Freiburg-im-Breisgau where it occupied one of the cells of a nun. The Cleveland sculpture measures 92.7 cm in height.

2. Peter Brown, *The Cult of the Saints: Its Rise and Function in Latin Christianity* (Chicago: Univ. of Chicago Press, 1982), 5.

3. Gregory of Nyssa, *Encomium on Saint Theodore,* in J.-P. Migne, *Patrologia Graeca,* 46.

4. See Émile Mâle, *Religious Art in France, the Thirteenth Century: A Study of Medieval Iconography and Its Sources,* ed. Harry Bober (Princeton, N.J.: Princeton Univ. Press, 1984), 7–15.

5. Christopher de Hamel, *A History of Illuminated Manuscripts* (Boston: David R. Godine, 1986), 160; Roger S. Wieck, *Time Sanctified: The Book of Hours in Medieval Art and Life* (New York: George Braziller with the Walters Art Gallery, 1988), 101–2.

6. George Ferguson, *Signs & Symbols in Christian Art* (New York: Oxford Univ. Press, 1954), 271–75.

4. Mater Gloriosa: The Cult of Mary in the Middle Ages

1. K. Bihlmeyer, *Heinrich Seuse, Deutsche Schriften,* in *The Art of Devotion in the Late Middle Ages in Europe,*

1300–1500, Hank van Os (Princeton, N.J.: Princeton Univ. Press, 1994), 104.

2. The Seven Sorrows consist of the following grievous events in the life of the Virgin Mary: (1) the Prophecy of Simeon at the Presentation in the Temple; (2) the Flight into Egypt; (3) the disappearance of the twelve-year-old Jesus when he stayed behind to dispute with the learned men of the temple; (4) meeting Jesus as he carried his cross to Calvary; (5) keeping watch at the foot of the cross; (6) the Deposition, or removing of Jesus's body from the cross; (7) the Entombment of Jesus.

3. Scenes forming the Passion Cycle typically include, but are not limited to, the following episodes: the Road to Calvary, Christ stripped of his garments, the Crucifixion, the Deposition (Christ taken down from the cross), the Virgin bearing the body of her dead son (Lamentation), the Entombment, the Appearance of the risen Christ to his mother, the Ascension, Descent of the Holy Ghost.

5. Images of the Cross and the Crucifixion

1. See Gary Vikan, "Byzantine Pilgrims' Art," in *Heaven on Earth: Art and the Church in Byzantium*, ed. Linda Safran (University Park: Pennsylvania State Univ. Press, 1998), 229–66.

2. Henry Suso, *Little Book of Eternal Wisdom and Little Book of Truth*, trans. James M. Clark (London: Faber and Faber, Ltd., 1953), 55, 58.

3. As cited by Jennifer Speake, *The Dent Dictionary of Symbols in Christian Art* (London: J. M. Dent, 1994), ix.

Glossary

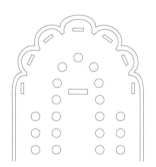

apse with ambulatory

basilica

ALTARPIECE: A painted picture or sculpture in relief representing a religious subject and suspended in a frame behind the altar of a church. The altarpiece is often made up of two or more separate panels created by a technique known as panel painting. It is then called a diptych, triptych, or polyptych, depending on whether it has two, three, or more panels. Groups of statuary can also be placed on the altar. Normally the altarpiece is set on the altar itself. Altarpieces vary greatly in size and conception and often include architectural encasement. See also *reredos, retable,* and *winged altarpiece.*

AMBULATORY: A passage or walkway that runs around the apse of a church.

AMPULLA: A small vessel, typically a flask or phial, used by pilgrims to carry sanctified oil, water, or earth from a holy site. Small ampullae, usually made of lead or clay, were worn around the neck and featured religious images of the sites visited by the pilgrim.

ANASTASIS: The Orthodox image for the Resurrection and depicting Christ's descent into Hell. He stands on its shattered gates and brings back to life Old Testament figures. For the Orthodox Church it symbolizes the salvation of mankind.

ANTEPENDIUM: A covering for the front of an altar.

ANTIPHONS: In the Roman liturgy, a responsory by a choir or congregation. In Gregorian chant, these were normally to a psalm.

APOCRYPHA: Various religious writings of uncertain origin; works of doubtful authorship or authenticity; also, a group of fourteen books, not considered canonical, included in the Septuagint and the Vulgate as part of the Old Testament.

APSE: A semicircular or polygonal extension to a church building, typically the east end of a church or its transepts.

ASPASMOS: A salutation or greeting. In Orthodox worship, normally expressed through touching or kissing.

AUREOLE: An oval or elliptical aura of light which, in Christian art, envelops an entire figure to express the radiance of sanctity. In the earliest Christian art this was extended exclusively to the three persons of the godhead but was afterwards extended to the Virgin and to several saints.

BALDUCCHINO (OR BALDACHIN): A canopy of state over an altar or throne.

BASILICA: An early Christian or medieval church especially common in Italy; typical features include a long nave with two or four aisles, a semicircular apse at the east end and a narthex at the west.

BEMA: The sanctuary of an Orthodox church.

BOOK OF HOURS: Prayer books intended for lay use in private or family devotions, typically containing a compendium of prayers and devotions dedicated to the Virgin Mary and recited or sung at the canonical "hours" of the day (eight set periods of the day). To this core were appended other elements such as a calendar, Penitential Psalms, litanies, and suffrages. Elaborate versions contain a full cycle of miniatures as well as involved marginal decorations. Books of hours form the most popular and abundant category of all surviving medieval manuscripts.

BREVIARY: Liturgical book comprising hymns, readings, psalms, anthems, and other prayers for the reading of the Daily Office, required of all priests, monks, and nuns.

BYZANTIUM: Historically, the Byzantine Empire, a classically based Christian civilization in existence for over a thousand years, which spanned the inauguration of its capital and intellectual center, Constantinople, in 324 to the fall of the city to the Ottoman Turks in 1453; the borders of Byzantium changed significantly over time, but the Byzantines considered themselves the inheritors of the Roman Empire from which it evolved.

CHI RHO MONOGRAM: The first two letters (XP) of "Christ" in Greek combined into a monogram.

CHOIR: The part of a church where services are sung; the eastern arm of the church between the crossing and the apse.

CHOIR SCREEN: An ornate barrier constructed of wood, stone, or metal separating the chancel from the nave and serving a similar function to the iconostasis in Orthodox churches; they are common in England where they are also called rood (referring to a cross that surmounted them) or chancel screens. See also *templon*.

CIBORIUM: A canopy with a domed or pyramidal upper structure resting on columns and covering the shrine where the Eucharist is kept; also an ornamental receptacle, typically of precious metal, for holding the Eucharistic bread.

COMPLINE: See *Daily Office*.

COPE: Cape worn in processions by the celebrant of the Mass; a semicircular vestment fastened across the chest by a brooch called a Morse.

COUNTER-REFORMATION: A period of renewal and reform within the Catholic Church extending from the papacy of Pius IV in 1560 to approximately 1648. Such reforms were introduced to counteract the rise of Protestantism and corruption within the church itself. Reforms included the training of clergy, the renewal of spirituality, and the proper forms for liturgy and church music.

CROSSING: The central space within a church located at the intersection of the nave and the transepts. The crossing is usually surmounted by a tower or dome.

CRUCIFIX: A cross with a representation of the body (or corpus) of Jesus attached to it; a principal symbol of the Christian faith and Christ's sacrifice for humankind by his death on the cross.

CRUCIFORM: A form in the shape of a crucifix, such as a cruciform plan church.

CULT: In the academic study of art and religion, a reference to a highly intense level of devotion by the faithful to a sacred person or group (as to the Virgin, the saints, and martyrs).

DAILY OFFICE (ALSO DIVINE OFFICE): A complex round of prayers and readings formulated for recitation at the "canonical" or "liturgical" hours of the day and required of all clergy, monks, and nuns. They are: Matins (about 2:30 A.M.), Lauds

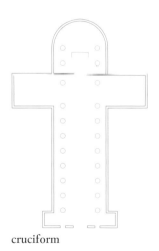

cruciform

(5:00 A.M.), Prime (6:00 A.M.), Terce (9:00 A.M.), Sext (noon), None (3:00 P.M.), Vespers (sunset), and Compline (9:00 P.M.).

DALMATIC: A sleeved tuniclike upper garment worn principally by deacons as their liturgical dress, but also worn by bishops and priests. The celebrant of the Mass wore this vestment under the chasuble.

DEISIS: A representation of Christ flanked by the Virgin and Saint John the Baptist in intercession, sometimes including other holy persons.

DIPTYCH: A painting of two panels hinged together so they open and close like a book; generally made in small scale for portability and private devotional use.

DIVINE OFFICE: See *Daily Office*.

diptych

DOGMA: The infallible teaching of a truth by the church concerning faith or morals, the belief of which is required of all Christians.

ECCLESIA AND SYNAGOGUE: Common allegorical figures in the art of the Middle Ages representing the transition from the Old Law to the New. They are rendered as draped females. Ecclesia (the New Law) typically wears a crown, carries a cross, and holds a chalice, representing the Redeemer's blood. Synagogue (Old Law) is always a blindfolded figure, with the blindfold representing moral or spiritual blindness, sin, and ignorance. Often a crown falls from the inclined head of Synagogue and the Tables of the Law fall from her hands.

EVANGELIST SYMBOLS: See *Four Evangelists*.

FISH: A common symbol of Christ, especially in early Christian art and literature. The symbol derives from the initial Greek letters of the five words "Jesus Christ God's Son Savior," which spells fish.

FOUR DOCTORS OF THE ORTHODOX CHURCH: Eastern counterparts to the Latin Church Fathers, they consist of Saints Athanasius, Basil the Great, Gregory Nazianzus, and John Chrysostom. As bishops, they were represented in art wearing their Episcopal robes.

FOUR EVANGELISTS: The traditional authors of the Gospels: Saints Matthew, Mark, Luke, and John. In art they are often represented by their respective symbols: a winged man, a lion, a bull, and an eagle.

FOUR FATHERS OF THE LATIN CHURCH: Also known as the doctors or venerated teachers of the church, they consist of Saints Gregory the Great, Ambrose, Augustine, and Jerome.

FRESCO: A painting that is rendered directly onto a wall or ceiling. The technique involves the laying of colors onto fresh (or still damp) plaster.

GREEK CROSS: A cross with four equal arms, generally symbolic of the church rather than Christ or his sacrifice for humankind.

HALO: See *nimbus*.

HORTUS CONCLUSUS: The term, meaning "enclosed garden," was taken from the Song of Solomon (4:12) and interpreted by medieval theologians as referencing Mary's fruitfulness combined with her simultaneous and perpetual virginity. In medieval art, Mary is shown seated with her infant child in a lush and verdant garden enclosed by walls.

ICON: A term deriving from the Greek *eikon*, meaing "image." Specifically it refers to images of sacred figures, especially on painted panels but also on ivories, frescoes, and mosaics. Such holy images play a critical role in Byzantine and Orthodox liturgy, worship, and private devotion. Icons were popularly believed to possess special powers for healing and protection and were often physically venerated by the devotee. Icons provided a vehicle for direct communication with the holy figure represented, which distinguished them for Western devotional images.

ICONOCLASM: The movement in the Byzantine Empire against the use and veneration of sacred images. The period lasted, with intervals, from 726 until 843. The term is often extended to cover the destruction of religious images in the Latin West.

ICONOGRAPHY: The investigation and study of subject matter in the visual arts; the branch of art history that interprets a work of art through images and symbols, particularly as they relate to the historical context of the work.

ICONOSTASIS: The screen separating the sanctuary in an Orthodox church from the congregation and intended for the displaying of icons. The iconostasis separated the congregation from the domain of the clergy. In their most developed form, icons can be arranged in up to five tiers, or registers.

INTAGLIOS: A figure or design carved in negative relief beneath the surface of a gemstone.

KOIMESIS: In the Orthodox Church, the *koimesis* (Greek) is the equivalent of the Western Assumption. It refers to the Dormition (death) of the Virgin and, as one of the Twelve Great Feasts of the Orthodox Church, it is celebrated on August 15.

LAMB: A common symbol of Christ in religious art, it derives from its sacrificial role in the ancient world, including Hebrew religious rites; seen as a foreshadowing of the death of Christ as a sacrificial substitute for mankind.

LILY: A symbol of purity, it is especially associated in art with the Virgin Mary.

LITTLE OFFICE OF THE VIRGIN MARY: Modeled after the liturgy of the hours that the priests and faithful recited daily from the breviary. In the book of hours it formed the first third of the book and contained hymns, psalms, and readings arranged for recitation in praise of the Virgin Mary. It was often accompanied by a cycle of miniatures depicting events in Mary's life.

LOROS: In Byzantine art, the heavy stole worn by both the emperor and empress. Often studded with precious stones, it was usually arranged in the form of an X over the upper body.

MAN OF SORROWS: An iconographic type of the Christ of the Passion in which he is shown lifeless, in bust length, upright and naked, with his arms either hanging or crossed over his chest.

MANDORLA: The extended rays of the aureole are enclosed within an almond-shaped frame surrounding the body of a sacred figure; the mandorla is frequently used with depictions of Christ, especially the Last Judgment, and sometimes with the Virgin, as in representations of her Assumption.

MAPHORION: In Byzantine art, the long veil worn over the head and shoulders; the typical attire of the Virgin, whose *maphorion*, the most sacred relic of Constantinople, was enshrined in the Blachernai Monastery.

MOSAIC: The technique of creating decorative effects or pictorial representations by using small pieces of colored stone or glass called *tessarae*. In the ancient world, the Romans achieved luxurious mosaic floors for their palaces, villas, and public buildings. The Byzantines developed the technique further by using colored and gilded glass to create wall mosaics of sacred figures inside churches.

NARTHEX: The single-story porch of an Early Christian church.

NAVE: The principal aisled space of a church extending from the west portal to the choir, or chancel.

iconostasis

mandorla

nimbus

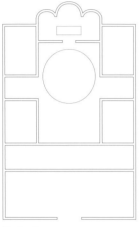

Orthodox

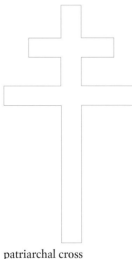

patriarchal cross

polyptych

NIMBUS: A halo. In religious art, the zone of light surrounding the head of a divine or sanctified person. Portrayals of God the Father, Christ, the Holy Spirit, and the Trinity generally incorporate a nimbus with rays of light emanating from the head within the circle of light. For depictions of Christ, a cruciform nimbus featuring a cross within a circle is used to represent redemption.

ORANT POSITION OF PRAYER: In the Early Christian Church, an attitude of prayer with arms extended sideways and upward.

ORTHODOX: The body of modern churches, including among others the Greek and Russian Orthodox, that is derived from the church of the Byzantine Empire (324–1453) and adheres to the Byzantine rite. The Orthodox Church acknowledges the honorary primacy of the patriarch of Constantinople and retains its own distinctive form of ecclesiastical architecture and art unique from that of the West.

PALLIUM: In the Roman Empire, an oblong outer garment of wool or linen worn over the tunic and draped over the left shoulder. It survives in Byzantine representations of figures in antique costume such as Christ, the apostles, and prophets.

PALM FROND: In art, the universal emblem or attribute of martyrs.

PANTOCRATOR: The image of Christ as all powerful and almighty. He is often enthroned, holding a book on his left knee and making a gesture of benediction with his right hand.

PASSION OF CHRIST: The suffering and death of Christ on the cross. In art, it refers to the events leading up to and immediately following the Crucifixion and may be conceived as single subjects or a sequence of narrative scenes.

PATRIARCHAL CROSS: A double cross, or one with two horizontal arms, originally designating the hierarchical rank of patriarchs and archbishops in the church.

PEACOCK: A symbol of immortality, especially in early Christian art.

PERIZONIUM: The band of cloth, or loincloth, worn by Christ on the cross to cover his nudity. The relic of the perizonium is said to be preserved in the Cathedral of Aachen in Germany.

PIETÀ: An image, found in both painting and sculpture, of the dead Christ accompanied either by angels or the Virgin. It is commonly a meditative form of the dead Christ lying on the knees of the Virgin.

POLYPTYCH: A painting consisting of four or more individual panels either hinged together or set into a fixed architectural frame as an altarpiece. It typically features a principal central image flanked by side panels with supporting images.

PREDELLA: The lower register or platform of an altarpiece or polyptych composed of smaller panels, often with subsidiary narrative scenes related to the main panels above and forming an appendage to them.

PRIE-DIEU: A private pew for an individual consisting of a kneeling rail and a shelf for supporting a book of hours or a psalter; commonly depicted in books of hours with the owner kneeling in prayer.

PROSKYNESIS: A gesture of supplication or deep reverance in Byzantine religious ceremonies. The physical act could involve full prostration to genuflection or a bow.

PSALTER: A book containing all 150 biblical psalms, used liturgically and for private devotion.

PTERUGES (OR PTERYGES): An apronlike element of armor worn by Byzantine cavalrymen to protect the upper thighs and midsection.

RELIQUARY: A shrine or container for the storage and veneration of a relic.

REREDOS: A screen immediately behind the altar of a church generally decorated with sculpted or painted religious images; in some churches these can be quite large. Related to the retable and often used in place of it, especially in high Anglican usage.

RETABLE: A painting or sculpted panel behind an altar, sometimes on a raised shelf and frequently including architectural encasement and part of the structure of a church. Some retables can be detached from the altar itself.

retable

ROOD SCREEN: The word "rood" derives from the Saxon word for cross. See *choir screen*.

SACRA CONVERSAZIONE: A composition found mainly in Renaissance painting in which several saints, regardless of the era in which they lived, are grouped around the Virgin and Child.

SANCTUARY: The area surrounding the main altar of a church generally reserved for the clergy.

SEVEN DEADLY SINS: A list of major sins identified by Gregory the Great in the sixth century. These eventually became standardized in the art and literature of the later Middle Ages: Sloth, Avarice, Anger, Envy, Gluttony, Lust, and Pride.

SEVEN JOYS OF THE VIRGIN: Happy events in the life of the Virgin Mary, a counterpart to the Sorrows of the Virgin and a set for devotion and contemplation. They include: the Annunciation, the Visitation, the Nativity, Adoration of the Magi, Presentation in the Temple, Assumption of the Virgin into Heaven, and Coronation of the Virgin. There is some variation to this list, and other events cited in art may include the Resurrection and Ascension of Christ and the Descent of the Holy Spirit at Pentecost.

SEVEN LIBERAL ARTS: A curriculum of education as defined in medieval cathedral schools and universities. It consisted of the *Trivium* (grammar, rhetoric, and logic) and the *Quadrivium* (geometry, arithmetic, astronomy, and music). Upon mastering these essential fundamentals of knowledge, the medieval student could then move on to the higher studies of theology, canon and civil law, and medicine.

SEVEN SACRAMENTS: Seven ceremonies said to have been instituted by Christ and entrusted to the church to convey grace and assist the faithful in the development of their spirituality and progress toward divine life. The Catholic Church lists them as follows: Baptism, Confirmation, Eucharist, Penance, Anointing the Sick, Holy Orders, and Matrimony.

SEVEN SORROWS OF THE VIRGIN: Grievous experiences in the life of the Virgin Mary: the Prophecy of Simeon, the Flight into Egypt, the disappearance of the young Jesus when he stayed behind to dispute the learned men of the temple in Jerusalem, meeting Jesus as he carried his cross to Calvary, keeping watch at the foot of the cross, taking down the body of Jesus from the cross, and the Entombment of Jesus.

SUBLIGACULUM: A kind of undergarment originally worn by ancient Romans. In Byzantine art the garment worn by Christ on the cross.

TAU CROSS: A cross shaped like the letter T, or *tau* in Greek.

TEMPLON: A low chancel barrier; in early Byzantine churches a low screen separating the sanctuary from the nave. It evolved into the later iconostasis still used in Byzantine churches today.

templon

THEOTOKOS: From the Greek referring to the Virgin Mary as the "God Bearer," or the Mother of God, as she is known in Orthodox Christianity.

triptych

tympanum

TRANSEPTS: The arms of a cross-shaped church extending to the north and south and meeting the nave at right angles to form the crossing.

TRANSUBSTANTIATION: During the consecration of the Eucharistic bread and wine by an ordained priest at Mass, the act whereby the elements are changed into the body and blood of Christ. The church teaches that an actual change of substance occurs and not a symbolic change.

TREE OF JESSE: The tree used to illustrate the human lineage of Jesus through the royal house of Judah to Jesse, the father of King David. A common motif in Western church decoration, typically showing a recumbent Jesse with a tree growing from his side with its branches extending to David, Solomon, the Virgin Mary, and the infant Jesus.

TREE OF KNOWLEDGE: The tree planted by God in Eden with a central role in the Fall. The tree plays an important role in Christian art and symbolism.

TRIPTYCH: A picture composed of three individual panels hinged together; the central panel is typically of larger size enabling the outer panels or wings to be folded over the central panel for protection; often made in small scale for portability and private devotion, but sometimes used on altars.

TYMPANUM: In medieval architecture, the semicircular space between an arch and above the lintel of a door; often filled with sculpture.

VIRGIN HODEGETRIA: "She who shows the way," an image of the Mother of God holding the infant Christ on her left arm and gesturing toward him with her right hand. Christ holds a scroll in his left hand and blesses with his right.

VIRGIN ORANS: An image of the Virgin depicted in the orant position of prayer with arms extended outward and upward.

WINGED ALTARPIECE: An altarpiece consisting of sculpture or painting in which the middle section has been attached to hinged wings that open and close. The primary (central) image was typically exposed on Sundays or feast days by opening the wings. Such altarpieces can have several pairs of wings that may be opened and closed in various combinations to expose different sacred images.

Bibliography

Alexander, Jonathan J. G. *The Painted Page: Italian Renaissance Book Illumination 1450-1550*, exhibition catalog. Munich: Prestel-Verlag, 1994.

Bandmann, Günter. *Early Medieval Architecture as Bearer of Meaning*. Trans. by Kendall Wallis. New York: Columbia University Press, 1998.

Bomford, David, and Jo Kirby. *Italian Painting before 1400*. London: National Gallery Company Limited, 2000.

Brown, Peter. *The Cult of the Saints: Its Rise and Function in Latin Christianity*. Chicago: University of Chicago Press, 1982.

Buckton, David, ed. *Byzantium: Treasures of Byzantine Art and Culture from British Collections*. London: British Museum Press, 1994.

Campbell, Gordon. *The Oxford Dictionary of the Renaissance*. Oxford: Oxford University Press, 2003.

Carr, Dawson W., and Mark Leonard. *Looking at Paintings: A Guide to Technical Terms*. Malibu, Calif.: J. Paul Getty Museum in association with British Museum Press, London, 1992.

Cormack, Robin. *Icons*. Cambridge, Mass.: Harvard University Press, 2007.

Cormack, Robin, and Maria Vassilaki, eds. *Byzantium 330-1453*, exhibition catalog. London: Royal Academy of Arts, 2008.

Cotsonis, John A. *Byzantine Figural Processional Crosses*. Washington, D.C.: Dumbarton Oaks, 1994.

De Hamel, Christopher. *A History of Illuminated Manuscripts*. London: Phaidon Press, 1994.

Ferguson, George. *Signs & Symbols in Christian Art*. New York: Oxford University Press, 1961.

Forsyth, William H. *The Pietà in French Late Gothic Sculpture: Regional Variations*. New York: Metropolitan Museum of Art, 1995.

Gambero, Luigi. *Mary in the Middle Ages: The Blessed Virgin Mary in the Thought of Medieval Latin Theologians*. San Francisco: Ignatius Press, 2005.

Grabar, André. *Christian Iconography: A Study of its Origins*. Princeton, N.J.: Princeton University Press, 1980.

Haering, Ilene E. *Cult Statues of the Madonna in the Early Middle Ages*. PhD dissertation, Columbia University, 1960. Ann Arbor, Mich.: University Microfilms, 1961.

Head, Thomas. *Medieval Hagiography: An Anthology*. New York: Garland Publishing, 2000.

Hourihane, Colum. *Objects, Images and the Word: Art in the Service of the Liturgy*. Princeton, N.J.: Department of Art and Archaeology, Princeton University, in association with Princeton University Press, 2003.

Kessler, Herbert L. *Seeing Medieval Art*. Peterborough, Ontario: Broadview Press, 2004.

Klein, Holger A., Stephen N. Fliegel, and Virginia Brilliant. *Sacred Gifts and Worldly Treasures: Medieval Masterworks from the Cleveland Museum of Art*. Cleveland: Cleveland Museum of Art, 2007.

Mâle, Émile. *Religious Art in France, the Thirteenth Century: A Study of Medieval Iconography and Its Sources*. Ed. Harry Bober. Princeton, N.J.: Princeton University Press, 1984.

Markow, Deborah. *The Iconography of the Soul in Medieval Art*. PhD dissertation, New York University, 1983. Ann Arbor, Mich.: University Microfilms, 1984.

Mathews, Thomas F. *Byzantium from Antiquity to the Renaissance*. New York: Harry N. Abrams, Inc., 1998.

Moorman, Msgr. George J. *The Latin Mass Explained*. Rockford, Ill.: Tan Books and Publishers, 2007.

Murray, Peter, and Linda Murray. *The Oxford Companion to Christian Art and Architecture*. Oxford and New York: Oxford University Press, 1996.

Nichols, Ann Eljenholm. *Seeable Signs: The Iconography of the Seven Sacraments, 1350-1544.* Woodbridge, UK: The Boydell Press, 1994.

Norman, Diana. *Siena and the Virgin: Art and Politics in a Late Medieval City State.* New Haven, Conn.: Yale University Press, 1999.

Olderr, Steven. *Symbolism: A Comprehensive Dictionary.* Jefferson, N.C.: McFarland, 1986.

Pelikan, Jaroslav. *Imago Dei: The Byzantine Apologia for Icons.* Princeton, N.J.: Princeton University Press, 1990.

———. *Mary through the Centuries: Her Place in the History of Culture.* New Haven, Conn.: Yale University Press, 1996.

Purtle, Carol Jean. *The Marian Paintings of Jan van Eyck.* PhD dissertation, Washington University, 1976. 2 vols. Ann Arbor, Mich.: University Microfilms, 1976.

Ross, Leslie. *Medieval Art: A Topical Dictionary.* Westport, Conn.: Greenwood Press, 1996.

Safran, Linda, ed. *Heaven on Earth: Art and the Church in Byzantium.* University Park: Pennsylvania State University Press, 1998.

Schiller, Gertrud. *Iconography of Christian Art.* 2 vols. Greenwich, Conn.: New York Graphic Society Ltd., 1971.

Speake, Jennifer. *The Dent Dictionary of Symbols in Christian Art.* London: J. M. Dent, 1994.

Talbot, Alice-Mary, ed. *The Oxford Dictionary of Byzantium.* 3 vols. New York: Oxford University Press, 1991.

Toman, Rolf, ed. *The Art of Gothic: Architecture, Sculpture, Painting.* Cologne: Könemann, 1999.

Van Os, Henk. *The Art of Devotion in the Late Middle Ages in Europe, 1300-1500.* Princeton, N.J.: Princeton University Press, 1994.

Vassilaki, Maria, ed. *Mother of God: Representations of the Virgin in Byzantine Art,* exhibition catalog. Athens: Benaki Museum; Milan: Skira Editore, 2000.

Verdon, Timothy Gregory, ed. *Monasticism and the Arts.* Syracuse, N.Y.: Syracuse University Press, 1984.

Warner, Marina. *Alone of All Her Sex: The Myth and the Cult of the Virgin Mary.* New York: Vintage Books, 1983.

Wieck, Roger S. *Painted Prayers: The Book of Hours in Medieval and Renaissance Art.* New York: George Braziller, Inc., 1997.

———. *Time Sanctified: The Book of Hours in Medieval Art and Life.* New York: George Braziller in association with the Walters Art Gallery, Baltimore, 1988.

Williamson, Paul. *Gothic Sculpture 1140-1300.* New Haven: Yale University Press, 1995.

Index

in, 97–98; cult of Mary in, 56, 58–59; images of Crucifixion in, 95–97
Miniature: Christ as Judge of the World, 38
Miniature from a Gradual: Initial G[audamus omnes in Domino], 50, 51
Miracle of Saint Anthony of Padua (Bening), 44, 44–45
monasteries/convents, 33–34, 50, 71
Monastery of Saint Catherine, Mount Sinai, 27, 32; paintings on wooden panels in, 25, 27
Monogram of Christ (Chi-Rho or Chrismon), 99
mosaics, 25, 29–30; depictions of Mary in, 27, 59–60; floor, 18
Mother Church, Mary symbolizing, 57–60, 62
Mother of God. *See* Virgin Mary
Mother of God, 27
murals, in churches, 28
mystics, art inspiring, 10

naturalism, 67, 93; in Byzantine Empire, 85; in depictions of Virgin and Child, 67; movement toward, 77–79; symbolism integrated with, 79
nave, proportions of, 28–30
Near East, 16, 49
Nero, 16
Notre-Dame de la Belle Verrière, 59
numbers/numerology, in ecclesiastical architecture, 15

paganism, 16, 20, 96
Painted Crucifix, 36
painting, *vs.* sculpture, 24
Palermo, mosaics in, 30
Palermo Cathedral, Gaggini sculptures in, 47
palm, as recurrent motif, 17–18, 48

Pantocrator, Christ as, 28–30, 37
paradise, in symbolism in Jonah Marbles, 23
the Passion: foretelling of, 65; Mary and, 56, 60, 75
patron saints. *See under* saints
patrons. *See* aristocracy/donors
Paul, Saint, 42, 42–43
peacock, as recurrent motif, 17–18
persecution, of Christianity, 16
Peter, Saint, 42; cues for identification of, 41–43; in depictions of Last Judgment, 38
philosopher, Christ as, 84
Piers Plowman (Langland), 99
Pietà, 60, 75
piety, artists', 81
Pilate, Crucifixion and, 90
pilgrims, ampullae of, 85–86, 86
Plaque from a Portable Altar with the Crucifixion, 97
Pórtico de la Gloria, 35
prayer: books of hours for, 38–40, 72–75; for clergy *vs.* laity, 38–40, 74; objects in, 31, 33; orant, 23. *See also* public/private worship; veneration
Procession of the Blessed Sacrament (Book of Hours of Queen Isabella the Catholic), 7
processions, votive objects carried in, 33
Prokopious, Saint, 28
public/private worship, 11–12, 23, 72, 75
purity: lily symbolizing, 68, 79; white symbolizing, 55, 67–68

Ravenna, 60; Church of San Carlino in, 19; Mausoleum of Galla Placidia in, 82; as seat of Byzantium, 18

realism. *See* naturalism
Redeemer, Christ as, 87–88
redemption. *See* salvation/redemption
Regina Coeli, Mary as, 60
Reims Cathedral, west facade of, 14
relics: in altar frontals, 19; Crown of Thorns as, 90; in cult of saints, 40; of True Cross, 86; Virgin's milk as, 65
renunciation, of the world, 55
the Resurrection, 12, 23, 55
Roch, Saint, 46–47, 95
Rodin, Nicolas, 72
Roger of Helmarshausen, 81
Rome, 20, 30, 90; art of, 16, 23–24, 28, 84; religion and, 16, 84

Sacra Conversazione (holy conversation), 69, 71–72
Sacra Conversazione (Memling), 71
sacrifice, redemption through, 88
Saint Jerome with the Lion, 45
Saint John the Evangelist, 43, 43–44
Saint Margaret, 47
Saint Roch, 46
saints, 10; cues in identification of, 41–48; in depictions of Virgin, 68–72, 76–77; Four Evangelists, 53–54; iconography of, 28, 31, 38, 48, 98; in images of Crucifixion, 93–95; litany of, 54; patron, 40–41, 47–48, 71; relics of, 19, 40; veneration of, 28, 31, 40
Salins, Guigone de, 72
salvation/redemption, 23, 68; Christ's blood in, 88–89; cross as symbol of, 80; Mary's role in, 58, 75
Santa Maria degli Angeli (Florence), 50
Satan, depictions of, 44, 47
Schlägel Altar, 84, 91

sculpture, 24, 65, 85; uses of, 9–10, 33
Seated Virgin and Child (de Werve), 65
Sebastian, Saint, 95
Second Coming, altars facing east to await, 13–15
Second Council of Nicaea, 27
Seven Sorrows of the Virgin, 61
shepherd, symbolism of, 20–22, 21
Silvestro dei Gherarducci, Don, 50
skull, Adam's, 88
Slavs, entering Christian Orthodox community, 32
Sluter, Claus, 65
soldiers, in images of Crucifixion, 88, 91
souls: symbolized by birds, 68; union with God, 35
Speculum historiale (Vincent of Beauvais), 41–42
sponge bearer, in images of Crucifixion, 88, 91
stained glass, Biblical history in, 3
Stephen, Saint, 48, 48
Suso, Henry, 60, 87–88
swords, symbolism of, 61
Swords of Justice, in depictions of Last Judgment, 38
symbolism: on altar frontals, 18–19; around Mary, 59–60; of color, 54–55, 67; of cross, 98; development of, 17–18; for Evangelists, 53–54; familiarity with hidden meanings of art, 98–99; of Immaculate Conception, 67–68; in Jonah Marbles, 20–23; realism and, 79, 85. *See also* iconography
Symeon Stylites, Saint, 30
symmetry, in architecture, 15
Synagogue, *vs.* Ecclesia, 97, 98
Synod of Cologne, 61